Contents

Introduction

Be careful! You are holding a very dangerous book in your hands! The pages that follow will encourage you to dig into a book filled with truths that will challenge your assumptions about your Christian faith and with exhortations that will call you to follow Jesus far out of your comfort zone. A book that, in short, challenges you to grow up.

That is really the focus of this epistle of James: encouraging immature followers of Christ to grow up in their faith and start living as Christ has called them to live. And that's a dangerous message to hear. If you are like me, you are probably pretty comfortable with where you are in your Christian life. Your faith is "under control." Of course, Jesus is important, but you don't let yourself get radical about following Him. Moderation in all things, after all, right?

If you are in that place, and you're happy being there, then I advise you to read no further. You should close this book now and don't pick it up again. Because in the pages that follow, as we walk through the teaching that this man James put down for us 2000 years ago, you will find yourself being challenged again and again. You will be challenged to be joyful in the midst of suffering. You will be challenged to seek Godly wisdom and to reject the wisdom of the world. You will be challenged to see others as God sees them, and to treat them accordingly. You will be challenged to tame your tongue and to consistently put into practice what you know to be true about how Jesus calls you to live.

You will be challenged to be mature in your Christian walk.

Because that is, overall, what James is calling us to be: mature. He wants us to be dissatisfied with our current level of righteousness; he wants us to desire to be daily more like Jesus, to be continually striving to know Him better and to make our lives look more like His.

That is a high, difficult calling, and it is not for the faint of heart. If you are not interested in having your Christian faith deeply challenged, you would be wiser to read something else.

But if seeking a deeper faith, if experiencing Jesus in a more real and profound way appeals to you, the I hope you will find ample encouragement in the pages that follow. I hope you will take seriously the high standards and expectations that James raises for us as followers of Jesus Christ. I hope that you will be encouraged by my efforts to expound what James is trying to teach us in his letter, and that you will be enabled to transform you life more into His likeness as a result.

If you've read my first "Missionary's Musings" book on Philippians, you know to expect that the chapters of this book began as a series of messages that I gave to the congregation of the International Christian Church of Yaoundé (ICCY) in Cameroon, where I continue to serve as one of the Elders. As with that first commentary, my hope is again that, by making these messages available in book form, the profound truths of James' letter might be an encouragement to you in your walk with Christ.

In case you are wondering, let me tell you just a little bit about myself. I am a missionary with Wycliffe Bible Translators, and have been serving in Cameroon (which is on the west coast of Africa, just south of Nigeria) since 1993. My job is to support the work of Bible translation in West Africa through children's education; I am trained as a high school English and drama teacher and I teach at Rain Forest International School in the capital of Cameroon, Yaoundé. I am married to a wonderful, Godly and beautiful woman, who is a far more wonderful helpmate than I deserve! God has blessed us with seven children; the oldest three have finished high school and are working their way into the adult world; the other four are still at home with us for a few more years. If you'd like to know more about us or the ministry of Wycliffe, look us up online at www.wycliffe.org.

Chapter One: From Whom and To Whom

James 1: 1

From James, a slave of God and the Lord Jesus Christ, to the twelve tribes dispersed abroad. Greetings![1]

Before beginning the series of sermons which form the chapters of this book, I had spent two years studying and speaking on the book of Ephesians, a very stretching and enlightening exercise for me. When I finished going through Ephesians, I began to look through the Scriptures to find another book that I could work my way through. At first, I was inclined to try Paul's two letters to Timothy; this made sense to me because Timothy was the pastor in Ephesus when Paul was writing to him, so that I thought there would be a beneficial continuity between those books and the study of Ephesians which I'd just finished.

But as I started to look into 1 Timothy, I found myself resisting it; though it is a great book (and I hope to come back to it at some point), still, it just wasn't speaking to me where I was at the time. So I turned in a totally different direction and started looking at the book of James.

This was a natural transition for me because I've always been fascinated by the book of James. It is rather the outcast of New Testament literature, for a number of reasons. First, it is written in a distinctly Hebrew style, a style which clearly mirrors the style of the wisdom literature of the Old Testament. It also makes very little mention of Christian theology or doctrine; in fact, it only twice mentions the name of Jesus at all. As Adam Clarke puts it, "had it not been for the two slight notices of our blessed Lord, we had not known it was the work of any Christian writer."[2] And even though it was likely the first of the New Testaments books to be written, still it was one of the last to be accepted as part of the cannon, largely because of its Jewish focus. It was well known to Jewish believers but the largely Gentile church of the third and fourth century which was debating which books should be included in the canon knew it only slightly. The Gentile churches of that day used it very little in their services, and many church leaders of that time argued that it was not actually inspired by God, and thus should not be included in the canon at all.

But the most significant hurdle this book has had to overcome is the accusation of heresy. Many church leaders over the centuries have felt that James contradicts some of Paul's central doctrinal positions, primarily Paul's emphasis on salvation through faith alone, not by works. In contrast, James focuses on salvation that comes through faith and is demonstrated by works, and emphasis which caused even Martin Luther to question its position in the canon.

James has had a rather difficult time over the years, and as we begin our study of this unique book, I'd like to start by focusing on several critical questions that have surrounded it, generating considerable controversy over the years.

Question One: James Who?

One of the most critical questions about this epistle has centered around the author. The letter starts out with this verse: **From James, a slave of God and the Lord Jesus Christ, to the twelve tribes dispersed abroad. Greetings!** Many of the commentators I read agreed that much of the controversy that surrounds this epistle could have been avoided entirely if only the author had properly signed his name!

The early church fathers were looking for something along the lines of "Paul, an apostle of Jesus Christ," or something like that, something that would have given them a solid clue as to who the author was. But "James, a slave of God and of the Lord Jesus Christ" doesn't really give us, two thousand years later, any meaningful clue as to who this James was.

That, of course, has not stopped people from speculating!

There are four New Testament figures named James who have been seriously considered as the author of this letter. The first is James, the son of Zebedee and the brother of John. He was one of the twelve apostles listed in Matthew 4:21 – 22 and, as far as we can tell, was one of the first four apostles to be called by Jesus (the others were his brother John and the brothers Peter and Andrew, who were called just before him). He was also one of the first apostles to be martyred when he was killed by Herod in about 44 AD.

The second candidate for authorship is James, the son of Alphaeus. He was another apostle, mentioned in the list of disciples found in Matthew 10:2 – 4. However, in spite of the fact that he made the list of the Twelve, we know almost nothing else about him; he was an apostle and that's about it!

We know even less about the next candidate, who is James, the father of the apostle Judas. His name is mentioned in the list of apostles found in Luke 6:15, noting him as the father of the apostle Judas. Likely, he is mentioned in this list simply to differentiate his son from Judas Iscariot, but other than the name of his son, we know absolutely nothing about this James.

And finally, the fourth candidate is James, the brother of Jesus, who is generally considered to be the most likely candidate for the author of this epistle. Though he was not a believer during Jesus' earthly ministry (as far as we can tell, none of His siblings were), apparently James got a special visit from Jesus after the resurrection. In 1 Corinthians 15:7 Paul writes, **"Then [Jesus] appeared to James, then to all the apostles,"** and for various reasons, most commentators believe Paul is talking about Jesus' brother. If that is true, then he is one of only two people (Peter being the other) who got personal visitations from the Risen Lord after the resurrection. In fact, several commentators make the assumption that it was because of this visit that James and the other brothers of Jesus came to be believers shortly after the resurrection, which explains why they were with the disciples in the upper room just before Pentecost in Acts 1:14.

Of these four possibilities, most Bible scholars eliminate the father of Judas and the son of Zebedee right at the start, the first because there is no evidence that he followed in his son's footsteps to become a believer himself, and the second, because he was martyred. The letter is generally believed to have been written between the late 40's (the most often suggested date is 48 AD) and about 62 AD; since James, the son of Zebedee was martyred by Herod in 44 AD, if he was the author, he would have been writing it at least four years after he died. This narrows the choice down to the son of Alphaeus and the brother of the Lord.

Some scholars have tried to simplify this problem by claiming that these two men are actually the same person, though that is rather hard to square with the fairly clear message in the Gospels that Jesus' brothers were not believers during His ministry[3] (not to mention that Jesus' brother would have been the son of Joseph). But there are some who have suggested this as a simplification of the problem.

But the unfortunate truth is we really can't get any further than this. We can make educated guesses and venture theories, but in the end, we just don't know exactly who this James was. As long as we're on this side of Heaven, the author's identity will likely remain a matter of conjecture and speculation.

Even so, if we accept the likely assumption that the author is the brother of the Lord, then there are several things that we know about him.

First of all, almost all Bible scholars agree that he was the James that Paul refers to in 1 Corinthians, which means we can be fairly certain that the person writing this epistle got a personal appearance from the Risen Lord shortly after His resurrection, even though the details of that visitation are not recorded for us in the Gospels. Second, he was well known, even outside of the Jewish community, as a great man of prayer. Historians of this period record that his knees were like the knees of a camel because he spent so much time kneeling in prayer.

Third (and probably most important, because this is how we know most of the other details refer to this James and not someone else), he was one of the early leaders of the church in Jerusalem. Remember, after Peter's miraculous escape from prison in Acts 12, he instructs the people in Mark's house to **"tell James and the brothers these things."** This seems to imply that even Peter deferred to James' position of authority among the early believers. Paul also mentions him in Galatians 2:9, where he lists him as one of the three pillars of the Jerusalem church; the others are Peter and John, but James is listed first, in the place of prominence. Then, in Acts 15, we read about the first council of Jerusalem, where the church wrestled with how to handle the question of Gentile believers. In this chapter, Peter speaks first, followed by Paul and Barnabas, who lay out their case. But then, James concludes, speaking almost as a moderator or leader, one who speaks with authority for the council when the final decision is made.

All of these facts imply fairly strongly that the author of this epistle was the head of the church in Jerusalem in the first few decades immediately following Christ's ascension and Pentecost.

What saves all of these details from simply being interesting historical facts is this. The author of this letter probably had the right to many titles of authority and honor within the early church. He may have been able to claim the title of apostle. He may have been able to claim direct blood kinship with the Lord Jesus. He almost certainly could have claimed the authority of the head of the church in Jerusalem, someone well known, well respected, one who had been singled out by the Risen Lord for a personal visitation.

With all of these titles and honors to choose from, what is the title that he uses to start his letter?

James, a slave of God and of the Lord Jesus Christ.

He could have been known for all of those great things: for his position, for his authority, for his reputation. But he wanted, instead, to be known as a servant of Jesus. That strikes me as very significant. As we begin to study this epistle, I hope that we can keep in mind this attitude. These are the words of a man who chose to find his identity wholly in his service to Christ. Though he had many other accolades that he could have relied on, that he could have used to puff himself up and make himself seem more important to his readers, instead, he wanted to be known by his service to his Lord.

That is an attitude that I know I should emulate much more than I do.

Question Two: Who is the audience?

The second main question or problem that this epistle has faced over the years is the audience. Verse one tells us that it was written, **"to the twelve tribes dispersed abroad."** The Greek word James uses here is *diaspora*,[4] which comes from a root word that means "to sow or scatter." It was the word regularly used to refer to the Jews who had been scattered among the nations at the time of the Babylonian captivity that had never been repatriated to Israel. When the time of captivity was over and the Jews were allowed to return home to Israel, some of them didn't; these were the *diaspora*.

So James is writing to the Jews who were living all over the known world, outside of Palestine. And that is the source of the trouble. The Jewish believers of the first three centuries knew this letter well. There is evidence that it was widely disseminated throughout the Roman world; pretty much wherever there were Jewish believers, we have found this letter.

But the church didn't remain primarily Jewish for very long; by the second century, many, or perhaps even most believers were Gentiles. And, understandably enough, the Gentile believers knew primarily the writings that were directed to them, such as the Gospel of Luke and the letters of Paul. They weren't as familiar with the letter of James, and they didn't use it much in their meetings. Thus, when the primarily Gentile church of the third and fourth centuries began to codify which books were inspired and deserved to be officially proclaimed as part of the canon of Scripture, James almost didn't make the cut! One of the requirements for inclusion in the canon that they looked at was that the work be in widespread use and acceptance among the churches, and the Gentile believers didn't pay much attention to James because it was written for the Jews.

Now, there are two ideas that strike me when I think about the audience James chooses. First, he is writing to outcasts. These Jewish believers really had no place in society. They lived among the Gentiles, but their laws and customs and everything about them kept them separate; that's what the laws and customs and culture of Judaism was designed to do! They weren't Gentiles, and the Gentiles often rejected them, simply because they were Jews.

But not only that, they were *Christian* Jews. They followed a Lord and Messiah that most Jews had rejected and refused to acknowledge. And at that time, most Jews had some pretty strong feelings about people who had chosen to follow Jesus. If you've forgotten how strongly they felt about this, just remember a guy named Saul, before God turned his life around. Because of their faith in Christ, these brothers that James is writing to were rejected, and often persecuted, by their fellow Jews as well.

These were the ultimate outcasts in society, accepted by no one outside of their own community of believers. As a result, many of them were very poor and almost certainly they were often oppressed by those around them. The book of James has a lot to say about suffering (he gets into that starting with verse 2), probably because his original audience knew what suffering meant. It strikes me that, if these words were meant to help and encourage those who were facing the kind of suffering that these first century Jewish believers were facing, then surely God can use those words in my life, when I face trials of my own!

I'm also struck by the implications of the word *diaspora*. As I said before, the base word means "to sow throughout" or "to scatter," which means this is, fairly obviously, an agricultural metaphor. Just as seed are scattered by the sower, so the Jews were scattered throughout the world. But I think James may have used this word, not simply because it was in common use to describe the scattered Jews, but also for a very specific, intentional reason. Because when you scatter seeds, they tend to grow where they are scattered.

This epistle was very likely written before most of the missionary journeys of Paul, so these Jewish believers who were sown throughout the nations were likely among the first converts that heard the Gospel from Peter on Pentecost. God had brought them together in Jerusalem and they heard the good news of salvation through Christ Jesus; they believed and became followers of Christ. And then, they went back to their homes and spread that good news to others. Thus, like seeds sown throughout a field, they were the seeds that God used to sow His Gospel throughout the world.

Maybe it's just the English teacher in me, but I like to think that James was poetically making a very important point here: he is acknowledging God's unbelievable sovereignty in orchestrating the spread of the Gospel hundreds of years before Jesus was even born. By allowing many of His people to remain in exile, He was making a way for the good news of Jesus to be scattered throughout the world, that all the world might come to know Jesus as their Lord and Savior.

Isn't it amazing to be reminded of the amazing power and awesome majesty of the God we serve?

Question Three: What is practical religion?

The final problem this letter has faced over the years is the topics that James addresses. I'm not going to spend much time here addressing this issue; that would make this a very long chapter and would leave me with very little to talk about in the rest of the book!

The one thing I do want to point out here is that James emphasizes a specific problem or need within the church that he was addressing this letter to. Different commentators have identified various different ways to quantify this problem. Warren Wiersbe suggests that James was writing against spiritual immaturity: these Jewish believers were simply refusing to grow up in their faith and so James wrote to them, exhorting them to gain spiritual maturity.[5] Charles Tyree, on the other hand, suggests that the problem was spiritual mediocrity: James had identified a great divide between what these Jewish believers confessed to believe and what their actions communicated about their true belief. Thus, James commands them to return to the path of righteous living, where the confession of their lives will be consistent with the confession of their mouths.[6] Various other commentators suggested that the focus was more general; this idea was expressed most succinctly in the phrase "practical religion." James wasn't concerned with religious thinking; rather, he wanted to lead people to a religion that was practical in shaping the lives of those who believed.

But the best summary, I think, was in the King James Study Bible. The editor calls James the Proverbs of the New Testament, which focuses on the themes of faith and works. James presents these ideas not as conflicting values but as complementary ideas that work together in a believer's life. Thus, he concludes, "the theme of James in not merely faith *and* works, but faith *that* works."[7]

That is the idea that really sums up what the book of James is all about, and it is these three idea that I want to leave you with as we close this first chapter. Like James, we ought to be people who find their identity no in our position or our abilities or our reputation, but rather in serving Jesus Christ. We ought also to recognize the sovereignty of God in putting us where He wants us to be for the furthering of His perfect plan, even when the place He has put us entails suffering for a season.

And finally, we ought to do all that we can to make sure our faith is not simply philosophical or theoretical. But rather, we must cultivate a faith that works, so that our lives might be transformed into the likeness of our Savior.

Chapter Two: To Lack Nothing

James 1: 2 – 4

My brothers and sisters, consider it nothing but joy when you fall into all sorts of trials, because you know that the testing of your faith produces endurance. And let endurance have its perfect effect, so that you will be perfect and complete, not deficient in anything.

One of the little known and (to my kids at least) quite amusing facts about me is that I was a wrestler in high school. That was consistently may favorite sport throughout my high school years. Now, at the start of my junior year, we got a new coach for our team. None of us knew anything about him, so we didn't really know what to expect when we showed up for the first practice at the start of the season. Coach Dion sat us down and explained how things were going to work that year. He told us that we would be practicing for two hours after school every day, which was pretty standard; we were used to that and expected it. Then, he told us that for the first hour, we would be running. In the second hour, we would work on skills, hold practice matches and other things like that, but for the first hour, we would be exclusively running.

And we were absolutely appalled! How on earth were we going to get ready to compete if we wasted a whole hour of practice every day on running? And of course, underneath that was the thought, "How are we going to *survive* an hour of running every day?" What on earth was this guy thinking?

But what could we do? He was the coach. So we showed up the next day, hoping we had misunderstood him, but sure enough, out we went for the first hour to run. We ran a mile or two around the track or sometimes across country. We would run up and down the steps of the bleachers or up and down the steps in the school. We ran all over the place! And while we ran, we cursed Coach Dion for every ache and pain we developed, just generally hating him for putting us through this useless torture and ruining our team.

Well, this went on for a few weeks and eventually, the day of our first match arrived. Now, at my high school, a wrestling match consisted of three two minute periods. And it is a pretty intense six minutes; you have to work pretty hard, going all out for the entire time, if you expect to consistently win. The match started and we went through our first period; at the end, we discovered that we were feeling pretty good, not very winded at all. Our opponents, on the other hand, were looking rather tired. The second period started and at the end, we were still feeling pretty good; a little bit tired, but still okay. Our opponents were downright winded. When we got to the third period, we were starting to feel rather tired; we started to have to push ourselves. Our opponents were exhausted; they'd been pushing themselves for a period and a half already, and they had nothing left to give.

Surprisingly enough, we won most of our matches that day. And some of us were wise enough to put two and two together. Overall, we had not won because we were stronger or faster or more skilled than our opponents. We were simply in better shape, and when they ran out of steam, we were able to keep going. Coach Dion had made us suffer to make sure we had the stamina we would need to last for the entire match. After that, we understood why we needed to take that time to run (though we still grumbled about it). It was unpleasant, but that trial was important because it was a critical step in helping us achieve our goal.

In the verses we're focusing on for this chapter, James talks about the importance of trials as well, and I'm willing to bet that some of those reading his letter back in the first century had trials to face that were slightly more significant than having to run for an hour every day. As Jews, they were the outcasts of the Roman world. No one particularly like the Jews and, at best, they were tolerated as long as they kept to themselves and didn't cause any trouble. So the people James was writing to were rejected by the general population around them. But, as Christians, they were also rejected by other Jews. The believed in a Messiah that their fellow Jews had rejected; in the larger Jewish community, their faith was considered blasphemy. As a result, they were oppressed and persecuted by everyone around them, making many of them very poor. They also lived in constant danger, almost always fearing for their lives. They had some serious trials to face.

And it is in this context that James writes the words of James 1: 2 – 4. He tells these oppressed, hated and downtrodden people, "**consider it nothing but joy when you fall into all sorts of trials**." I don't know about you, but to me that statement, written to people in the midst of almost constant and significant suffering, seems rather unsympathetic. I've known some people who have stood in the midst of some significant suffering; undoubtedly you have as well. When I think of great suffering, invariably I think of a couple I knew named Bob and Ruth Chapman. We served with them for several years here in Cameroon, and when we first met them, we heard the story of their two sons. They had been on furlough in Canada when their two boys both came down with malaria. And, because the doctors in Canada were unfamiliar with cases of malaria (and because both the cases were quite severe), both of their boys died, within an hour of each other. I can only imagine the kind of grief and suffering they were going through on that day, and I absolutely can't imagine someone coming up to them, in the midst of that insuperable grief, and announcing, "Well, your sons are dead. What an opportunity to rejoice!" Such a statement at such a time would have been incredibly insensitive.

But that's essentially what James is saying here: Consider it nothing but joy that you are facing the difficult and dangerous circumstances that you are now facing. What a great opportunity you now have to rejoice!

Obviously, there is more going on here than James being insensitive to his audience; there are some significant truths that James is trying to communicate to them in the midst of their suffering.

A Few Thoughts About Trials

But before we get into our examination of those truths, I want to take a quick look at what James says and what he implies about trials in these verses.

The first thing I notice is that we can count on trials coming. James says, **"Consider it nothing but joy** *when* **you fall into all sorts of trials."** Not *if* but *when*. There is a sense of inevitability about the coming of trials; we will experience them. That's a promise we have not only from James and several other New Testament writers, but also from Jesus Himself. And if you think about it, that makes perfect sense. We are in the midst of a spiritual battle, and we live our lives behind enemy lines, in occupied territory. Not too many soldiers go out to the battlefield and expect to face no difficulties or hardships; they expect to fight a battle and possibly be killed. It is rather foolish of us to imagine that we can stand against the ruler of this world and face no hardships or opposition. So, James affirms this basic truth of the Christian experience: trials will come; expect them!

Secondly, James tells us that we should expect trials of many different kinds; the trials that we will face will be various. The word translated as "all sorts" literally means "variegated," a word which, in its original sense, referred to a tapestry or some kind of cloth that was made up of many different colors woven together. And that is the idea James is aiming at here: our trials will be as various and different as the colors of the rainbow.

There are, I think, several implications of this idea. First, these trials can not be anticipated; they can come at any time in any form and there really isn't anything we can do to anticipate or avoid them. Which logically implies the second idea: James is referring here to trials that are not of our own making. He gets into the trials we create for ourselves in verse 13 of this chapter, which we will get to in due course. But the trials James is talking about in these verses are not the trials that come to us as a result of our own sinful or stupid decisions; these are the trials that are either common to all people or those that are particular to us as believers. And finally, because these trials are so unpredictable, we need, as Matthew Henry points out, to always have on the full armor of God.[8] We never know what we're going to be facing next, so we constantly need God's full armor to protect us completely, no matter what comes our way.

So, these trials will come and they will come in many different forms. The third observation I have is that James tells us we can count on these trials to be serious. The word translated as "fall into" means "to face on every side." The same word is used in Luke 10: 30 in the parable of the Good Samaritan: **"Jesus replied, "A man was going down from Jerusalem to Jericho, and fell into the hands of robbers."** And that is the idea behind this word, to be surrounded by, to be overwhelmed. James is not referring to trials of the "my alarm clock didn't go off and now I'm rushed to get to church on time" variety. No these are the other kind: the diagnosis of cancer; the accident that debilitates; the sudden death of a loved one; the loss of a job or a ministry through no fault of your own; the persecution from those who hate the Kingdom of God and who hate you simply because you claim the name of Christ. James tells us that these are the kinds of trials we can expect will come into our lives, unexpectedly, unavoidably; this is what we can expect in our Christian lives.

How to Deal with Trials

Recognizing that these kinds of trials are coming, James goes on to give his audience a recommendation on how we ought to deal with them when they come. And that advice is: Consider it nothing but joy! Rather strange advice, to say the least.

But what I find interesting is the words that James uses. The word translated "consider" is actually a noun, at least that is how it is most often used in the rest of the New Testament. As a noun, it means "prince" or "ruler" or "one who commands." So the first part of this verse could be translated, "Be ruled by nothing but joy." Given the word that he chooses, it seems clear that James is issuing a command here. This verse is not so much saying, "It would be nice if you consider," but rather "You *will* consider it nothing but joy!"

Undoubtedly there are many implications that could be drawn from this command, but I want to look at just one of those. By phrasing this statement as a command, James is teaching us something about the nature of trials, or, more specifically, about our reaction to trials. I'm reminded of a scene in the play *Cyrano de Bergerac*. In that play, the title character, Cyrano, is known for three things: his deadly skill with the sword, his fierce temper and his enormous nose. He can not endure anyone mentioning his nose (or even anything about any nose, for that matter) and his normal method of dealing with someone who is so foolish as to make such a comment is to attack them with his sword. Now, early in the play, Cyrano makes a foolish promise to the woman he secretly loves; he promises to protect a new member of his company, a young man named Christian. Unfortunately, Christian doesn't know about this arrangement and he enters the barracks determined to make a name for himself by showing his fellow soldiers how brave he is. And he does this by trying to pick a fight with the strongest solider in the group: Cyrano. So, as Cyrano is telling a story about one of his past exploits, Christian constantly interrupts him with references to his nose.

Normally, Cyrano would never have put up with this, but, because of his promise, he can't allow any harm to come to Christian (which, unfortunately for him, would include harm that he causes himself!). So, he simply has to endure Christian's taunting. In other words, Cyrano is facing a difficult trial and he has to make a choice: will he react with violence (his natural reaction) or will he honor his promise and endure.

James tells us that, when we face trials, we also have a choice to make. We can become defiant and rebellious. We can become despondent and give up in despair. We can begin to complain and feel sorry for ourselves, trying to encourage others to feel sorry for us too. Those are our natural reactions to suffering. But James' point is that becoming bitter or angry or despondent is not inevitable. It is easy, even natural, but not inevitable. Instead, you can choose to be joyful. And as a believer, you should choose to be joyful.

Which is all very well to say, but how does one actually do that? How can you stand in the midst of difficult struggles and choose to be joyful? How could someone like Bob and Ruth Chapman look back on the deaths of their boys and choose joy?

Warren Wiersbe suggests that it depends on what we know; we must choose to see our trials in the context of God's perspective on our lives, keeping in mind what we know to be true about God and about the trials themselves.

And what is it, specifically, that we know? James tells us, **"because you know that the testing of your faith produces endurance**." Now, in this statement, I see James communicating two specific truths. First, trials test our faith. The word translated as "testing" refers to the process of smelting precious metals, specifically gold. The gold ore was heated until it melted, at which point, anything that wasn't gold, any impurities, would rise to the top as dross and could be skimmed off. And after this process was repeated many times, you would be left with pure gold, something infinitely more valuable than what you had to start with.

I find this to be a fascinating and powerful image. Apparently during Biblical times, during the refining process it was impossible to tell exactly how much impurity was left in the metal. They did know, however, that gold was very reflective and the dross was not. So the smelters would watch the molten gold carefully, and once they could see their reflection in it, they knew the gold was getting pure. In the same way, God is watching our lives carefully, waiting to see His reflection in us. This is the kind of test James is talking about here, testing that refines our faith, that allows God to strip away the things in our lives that are impure and that block our ability to reflect His image in our lives.

Now, this is a rather general interpretation drawn from the use of this particular word; a valid interpretation, I think, but still, a very general one. But verse three is not a general statement; it is very specific and pins down exactly what God uses these trials for in our lives: to produce endurance. And here again, James uses a very precise word, which means "the ability to endure, to continue on in a task." Picture someone carrying a heavy load for a long time. The one with perseverance will not give up halfway; they will carry the load to the finish, regardless of how heavy it is or how weary they are. The person who perseveres will accomplish what they set out to do. In using this particular word, James is suggesting that trials are used by God to develop in us that ability to continue on in our Christian walk, no matter what happens.

But this rather begs the question of *why* this kind of perseverance is so important for us to have. Wiersbe suggests that "God wants to make us patient[9] because that is the key to every other blessing." Matthew Henry suggests that such perseverance shows our ability to trust in God's faithfulness when we wait on Him in all circumstances, so that we are neither running ahead of Him nor dragging our feet behind as He leads. [10] Some Old Testament saints struggled to learn this lesson, like Abraham, when he couldn't bear to wait for God's perfect timing and had a child with Hagar; just think of all the strife and hardship that the world has endured, even down to the present day, which can be traced back to that single act of impatience! Or, on the opposite end, is Jonah; remember how put out he was that the people of Nineveh repented? He was angry at the plant, angry at the worm, angry at the sun, and, most of all, angry at God. Those final verses of the book of Jonah always remind me of a spoiled child when they don't get their way; that's how Jonah was acting: like an immature child!

The Mark of Maturity

And in the end, I think that is what this whole passage is really all about: spiritual maturity. The kind of patience or perseverance that James is talking about here is one of the hallmarks of spiritual maturity. As Wiersbe puts it, "immature people are always impatient; mature people are patient and persistent." He even takes this one step further, suggesting that impatience and unbelief usually go together, as do patience and faith.

Which makes sense, I think. We serve a mighty God who is able to save us from any trials we might face. The more we believe that, the more able we are to patiently await His perfect timing; conversely, the less we believe in Him and the more we rely on our own strength, the more impatient we will be with our circumstances.

So James is showing his readers, and us, one of the basic marks of a mature Christian: one who perseveres, who is content to wait for God's perfect timing. That is why, in verse four, he tell us, **"let endurance have its perfect effect, so that you will be perfect and complete, not deficient in**

anything." This does not mean, of course, that as soon as we become patient we will suddenly find ourselves perfect and without sin. But it does mean that being content to wait on God's timing is one of the crucial lessons we must learn on our journey toward perfection. To quote Wiersbe one more time, "When the believer learns to wait on the Lord, God can do great things for him."

And that is a lesson so important for us to learn that God is willing to allow trials to come into our lives so that we can learn it, because this particular lesson can be learned in no other way. My wrestling coach in high school knew that the only way we could gain the endurance we needed was to go through the painful process of regularly exercising. In the same way, spiritual endurance comes only through facing and patiently waiting on God through difficult circumstances.

It is this principle that James is trying to lay out for us in this passage. You face trials because God wants you to be perfect, and that perfection comes through learning to trust and wait on Him. To learn to wait on Him, you have to learn to persevere, no matter what. So these trials that lie before you are the mark, the proof of God's continued work in your life for your sanctification. So consider it nothing but joy as you face them, because when God is through with you, you will be perfect, complete, not lacking anything.

This lesson is as true for us today as it was in the first century. When you find yourself in the crucible of life, remember what that means. God is purifying you so that you will be able to reflect His perfect image more clearly in your life.

So consider it nothing but joy!

Chapter Three: Asking for Wisdom

James 1: 5 – 8

> **But if anyone is deficient in wisdom, he should ask God,
> who gives to all generously and without reprimand, and it
> will be given to him. But he must ask in faith without
> doubting, for the one who doubts is like a wave of the sea,
> blown and tossed around by the wind. For that person must
> not suppose that he will receive anything from the Lord,
> since he is a double-minded individual, unstable in all his
> ways.**

In the first four verses of his epistle to the Jews who are scattered throughout the Roman world, James focuses on trials and hardships. This makes sense, considering his audience consisted of some of the poorest, most downtrodden people in the ancient world, hated by both Jews and Gentiles alike. James encourages these struggling believers to rejoice in their sufferings, because God was using those trials to help them reflect His image more perfectly.

Then, in the next four verses, he rather abruptly changes gears. As you can see from verses 5 – 8 of chapter one (printed above), he begins talking about wisdom.

Now, I don't know how the Jewish believers who originally read this letter reacted to the statements James makes in these verses, but if it had me, I'd probably have been thinking, "What do you mean ask for *wisdom*? How about a job? How about food for my family? How about relief from the trials and persecution we're facing? Those are the things we lack, not wisdom!" I find it rather interesting that James doesn't appear to even consider those other needs, needs which, to me, seem most pressing. That would seem to imply that God's priorities, God's opinion of what is most important for us to have, what we most need, is rather different than mine.

There is no doubt that the people James is writing to needed many things. But the only thing James is inspired by God to encourage them to seek is wisdom.

The Importance of Wisdom

So what exactly is wisdom and why might it be so important? Being an English teacher, I always like to start with definitions. The Greek word that James uses for wisdom is *sophia*, which is one of four Greek words that expressed the concept of wisdom. The others include the ideas of general knowledge, just knowing "stuff," understanding concepts andn being able to recognize connections between ideas. But all of these other words are specific applications of the broader, more general word *sophia*.

Sophia is a complicated word to define because it is used to mean many different things in Scripture, but there are three basic definitions that I found. *Sophia* means: 1) insight into the true nature of things; 2) wisdom as exhibited in action; and 3) mental excellence of the highest sense (in this final sense, Scripture uses it to describe the wisdom of God in perfectly ordering all the events of history).

If that is what *sophia* means, then what James says in verse five seems like a pretty tall order. I mean, how many of you can confidently say you have that kind of wisdom? That you have the ability to see the truth in any circumstance (parents, wouldn't *that* be useful to have!)? That you have the ability to act wisely all the time, with full knowledge and understanding of the consequences of your actions? That you are able to order your life, as much as it depends on you, just as God orders the events of history for the fulfillment of His will?

I have to picture the scene as this letter was first read. As the pastor stood at the front of the church and read James' words, "If anyone is deficient in *sophia*…" how many of those listening responded, "Nope, I'm good. I've got that covered"? Probably not too many, because this word *sophia* covers a concept that is just way beyond human ability; *nobody* has wisdom like this!

Which brings up two interesting points. The way James phrases verse five seems to indicate that this kind of wisdom is something we *ought* to have. He appears to expect that there should be some in his audience who *can* say, "Nope, I've got this covered," and he is simply talking, in this verse, to anyone who, for some reason, might not. He says, **"But *if anyone*…"** That strikes me as an interesting expectation that, as believers, we ought to be wise in such a way.

Secondly, James seems to be indication that this kind of wisdom is something that we need. He doesn't say, "If anyone wants to have wisdom," or "If you think wisdom might be good for you…." No, he says, **"If anyone is deficient in wisdom…."** The word translated as "deficient" in the Greek means "to be wanting, to be destitute of"; the connotation is that you are missing something that is necessary, something vital to your existence. In fact, it is the same word he uses in verse four when he describes how perseverance will make us mature and complete, not deficient in anything. So this verse is really saying, "If anyone is destitute, desperately in need of wisdom…"

I don't know about you, but I find this rather troubling. James expects that some of us ought to wise in this way and that those of us who aren't desperately need to be. That troubles me, because, when I was researching this passage and discovered the definition of *sophia*, my first reaction was neither, "Yeah, I've got wisdom like that" nor "Wow, that's exactly what I need; where do I get that?" No, my reaction was more along the lines of, "Yeah, right! That would be nice to have, but be realistic! *Nobody* is wise like that!" This is the kind of wisdom that I could never hope to have!

So this expectation of James', that we should have and greatly need this kind of wisdom, made me start to wonder. Why do we need this kind of wisdom? I mean, if truth be told, I think most of us generally feel like we're wise enough as we are. Until I'm facing the consequences of one of my monumental blunders, or until I start reading verses like this, I don't generally spend a lot of time lamenting how foolish I am; in fact, when I think about it at all (which is probably far too often), I generally think of myself as rather wise, and I suspect I'm not entirely alone in that.

But James seemed fairly convinced that we do need this kind of wisdom (which I obviously do not have, regardless of the comfortable feeling I normally have about my own wisdom), which made me start to wonder why. I'm not the first to wonder about this, of course. Many of the commentators that I read had also wondered, and they came up with several different theories about how to answer this question. Some suggested that we need wisdom in order to understand the trials that God is using to build perseverance in our lives, a suggestion that makes sense, given the context of the passage. Others thought the wisdom being referred to is more general, implying that we are simply too foolish for our own good and we need this wisdom James mentions in order to survive. Still others attributed this focus on wisdom to the Jewish love of wisdom in general, which hearkens back to God's affirmation of Solomon when he asked for wisdom rather than riches or long life. Ever since then, the Jews have held wisdom in high regard, and these commentators suggested that James is simply carrying that tradition on into the Christian era.

Any one, or maybe even all of these idea might have some truth in them. But I was struck by another possible answer, one that is found in the second half of verse five: **But if anyone is deficient in wisdom, he should ask God… and it will be given to him.** This may seem rather simplistic, but one thing I hear James saying is that we should get wisdom, this *sophia* wisdom *because we can*! It is openly available to anyone, free for the asking, so why wouldn't you go and get it?

Maybe I'm struck by this idea because of my original reaction to verse five. When James tell us we need *sophia* wisdom, I scoff. I shrug off this command as impossible even in the midst of reading the verse that tells me I can have it just by asking. In other words, I am content to rest in the wisdom I already have rather than seek after this *sophia* wisdom that God promises to give, if only I will ask. This reminds me of a concept C. S. Lewis expresses in *The Weight of Glory*. He is discussing joy, but I think it still applies here as well. He says we are, "like an ignorant child who wants to go on making mud pies in a slum because he can not imagine what is meant by the offer of a holiday at sea. We are far too easily pleased."[11]

Maybe I'm the only one who reacted this way, but it seems to me that there is a danger of being too easily pleased with the wisdom we have in our own strength. James encourages us not to be satisfied, but rather to see the incredible wisdom that God willingly offers.

How to Gain Wisdom

This, of course, brings up the practical question: How do we get this kind of wisdom? The short answer, which we've already mentioned, is, of course, to ask. Pray that God will give you this *sophia* wisdom and He will. Just ask for it and it's yours, no strings attached.

Well, maybe one string. Verse six says "**But he must ask in faith without doubting.**" I like the way the New Living Translation puts this idea: "**But when you ask him, be sure that you really expect him to answer.**" And unfortunately, that is a pretty big string.

The commentators I read had a lot to say about this concept. For example, Adam Clarke says "Never suppos[e] that God will permit [a man] to ask in vain, when he asks sincerely and fervently. Let him not hesitate, let him not be irresolute."[12] Matthew Henry comments, "There must be no wavering, no staggering at the promise of God through unbelief, or through a sense of any disadvantages that lie on our own part."[13] Or, there is William Burkett's idea, that "the manner of asking must be faithful, with a pure intention of God's glory, with cheerful submission to God's will, with fiducial recumbency[14] upon God's promise with great fervency and warmth of spirit."[15]

After reading all of these ideas, I found myself no longer surprised that I don't yet have this kind of wisdom. Because I would summarize all of these ideas simply as this: you must have absolutely perfect faith, without a shred of doubt, or you will receive nothing from God. But in my mind, if wisdom is only given to one who asks in perfect faith, then this is a rather empty promise. It would mean that only the wisest of men can petition God in perfect faith, and only the one with perfect faith can petition God to become the wisest of men. If this is true, it is no wonder that Solomon remains in a class by himself!

But then I read the commentary of Albert Barns, and his conclusion about wisdom was this:

> We may come to him with the utmost confidence, the most entire assurance, that it will be granted. In this case, we should come to God without a doubt that, if we ask with a proper spirit, the very thing that we ask will be bestowed on us. We cannot in all other cases be so sure that what we ask will be for our good, or that it will be in accordance with His will to bestow it; and hence we cannot in such cases come with the same kind of faith.... Here, however, nothing prevents our coming with the assurance that the very thing which we ask will be conferred on us.[16]

The idea I get from Barnes is this: in all other requests that we make of God, there is a chance that what we are asking for is not really what we need. In fact, there's almost always a fairly good chance that it is not what we need. But God desires for us to be wise and He is eager to "**give to all generously and without reprimand**." So when we ask for wisdom, we know we are asking according to His will, and thus we can be completely confident that He will grant our request.

But if that is the case, why does James spend the next two verses talking about the "double-minded individual"? As James describes him, this is the one who asks faithlessly, who can expect to receive nothing from God. I think the answer to this question lies, at least partly, in verse five. One commentator[17] noted that the Greek phrase in verse five translated "but he must ask," is in the present active imperative tense. That means that a literal translation of this phrase would be "he must keep on asking continually." The point is, asking God for wisdom is not a one time deal. James did not expect or suggest that God would answer our request immediately, once for all. No, when we ask for wisdom, God generally answers by placing us in circumstances where we can gain it, usually difficult circumstances, where we can learn to more fully rely on Him, which is the beginning of wisdom. The trouble is, in times when we are facing difficult circumstances, we tend to be most likely, most strongly tempted to rely on our own strength and our own wisdom rather than turning to God. Just think of the Israelites at the foot of Mount Sinai when Moses was delayed at the top, receiving the Ten Commandments. The people knew Moses had gone up to speak with Go and that he was going to bring God's Word s and wisdom down to them when he returned. But they couldn't wait, and turned instead to the golden calf that they made. Things didn't turn out so well for them when Moses got back, did they?

But it is the same for us today. In the midst of trials, we find ourselves being tossed back and forth, sometimes trusting wholly in God's strength, sometimes looking to our wisdom to see us through; sometimes desiring with all our hearts the holy life that God offers, sometimes craving the sinful lusts of our flesh. We are unstable, going back and forth like the waves of the sea.

The word "double-minded" that James uses in verse eight really sums up this idea well. It is a rather interesting word, found nowhere else in any older Greek literature, which leads some experts to believe that James coined it here in his epistle. It is a compound word formed from two smaller words. The first of these means "twice" and the second means "soul." So literally, James is talking about a two-souled man, one who is seeking to give his heart and his life to two masters at the same time. Jesus made it fairly clear in the Sermon on the Mount that trying to live that way never works. So the double minded man that James is describing is seeking to serve God with his whole heart while, at the same time, trying to maintain control of his own life. Such a man would most certainly be unstable in all his ways. The word translated as "unstable" is the negative form of a word that means "to set in order." So

James is saying that this person's whole life is in disarray.

And I think it is important to note the progression that James goes through here in these verses. You should ask for wisdom and God will happily grant it if you do. But you should ask in faith, trusting that God will grant your request, because only someone trusting in something other than God would be unable to ask for wisdom in faith; such people are double-minded and, as a result, their lives are a wreck. When they face difficulty or trials, they have nothing to hold on to and thus they're tossed about like the waves of the sea.

The Conclusion of the Matter

So where does all of this leave us? What conclusion should we take away from all of this?

One likely conclusion that occurs to me is that we should avoid asking for wisdom, because when we do, God will likely send trials and our faith might not be up to the task! But I'm not sure that is the message I want you to walk away with today.

And I'm fairly sure that isn't the message that James intended to communicate in these verses either. To him, the trials that inevitably come through our lives are God's gift to us, opportunities for us to be molded further into His perfect image. If we just trust that He is able to supply all our needs, and as we learn to trust Him in the midst of difficulty, then we begin to grow in the *sophia* wisdom that He greatly desires to give us.

So ask, if any of you lacks wisdom. Ask God, who gives to all generously without reprimand, and it will be given to you.

Chapter Four: The Poor and the Rich

James 1: 9 – 11

> **Now the believer of humble means should take pride in his high position. But the rich person's pride should be in his humiliation, because he will pass away like a wildflower in the meadow. For the sun rises with its heat and dries up the meadow; the petal of the flower falls off and its beauty is lost forever. So also the rich person in the midst of his pursuits will wither away.**

As I begin writing this chapter, I feel like I ought to start with a disclaimer: In this chapter, I'm going to be talking about money.

Money is a dangerous topic to mention in Christian circles, particularly in church, because as soon as you mention money, people immediately assume that you are asking for more of it, saying something along the lines of, "The offering baskets aren't full enough, so we're going to send them around again – let's fill them up this time!"

But even outside of the church, money is a topic that tends to make many Christians uncomfortable. We seem to have a sense that we ought not to focus our attention on money, and often times, that is quite true. But, of course, to a certain extent we have to focus on it, because we have to have it to live.

In some ways, I think those of us who are in full time Christian ministry struggle with this the most, because we're forced to spend a lot of time thinking about money, particularly when we head back to our home countries for furloughs. One of the major issues my wife and I have to contend with during those times of furlough is always deputation: finding people (or more people, as the case usually is) who will support us financially so that we can continue our work here in Cameroon. It is a focus that we find very uncomfortable and, at times, quite frustrating, because it feels like a constant distraction from what we feel like we should be doing.

But the Biblical writers were not nearly as shy on this subject as we tend to be in the modern church; they had a great deal to say about money! The Law of Moses has very detailed regulations about lending money and the practice of usury, or charging interest for money that has been lent. And the Law clearly establishes (in fact, it goes on at great length about) God's requirement for His people to give back a tithe of their wealth to the Lord. The wisdom literature of the Old Testament is also full of exhortations about money. We are admonished in Ecclesiastes 5:10 that, **"The one who loves money will never be satisfied with money, he who loves wealth will never be satisfied with his income."** Proverbs 13:11 tells us, **"Wealth gained quickly will dwindle away, but the one who gathers it little by little will become rich."** And in Psalm 15, the proper use of money is listed as one of the characteristics of the righteous; it is one of the marks of the one who may dwell in the sanctuary of the Lord.

This is not a purely Old Testament opinion either; in the New Testament Jesus has a great deal to say about money as well. In fact, many of His parables deal with the wise, or sometimes unwise, use of money as a way to teach many things about how we should live as children of God. Remember also, it was Jesus who drove the money changers out of the Temple, implying that greed is perhaps a bad thing. And of course, there is His famous and oft quoted words in Matthew 6:24: **"No one can serve two masters… You cannot serve God and money."**

Keep in mind, this is just a small selection of the verses in Scripture that specifically use the word "money." If you look up words like riches, wealth, prosperity, you will find literally hundreds more. The bottom line is, the Bible has a great deal to say about the subject of money.

And it is in the context of this vast store of Biblical wisdom concerning money that James makes the first of several comments on this subject in his letter, beginning with verses 9 – 11 of chapter one (printed above), and it is these verses that I want to focus on in this chapter.

Be Proud

Now, the first thing that jumps out at me in this passage is the word "pride." James tell both the rich and the poor that they ought to take pride in their position. But wait a minute! Isn't pride a bad thing? I've heard pastors suggest that pride is the only real sin, that all other sins ultimately stem from our prideful desire to be our own god, our desire to be able to live without relying on God. So what is James doing, suggesting here that we *ought* to be proud?

Unfortunately, in this case going back to the Greek doesn't really help all that much. The word James uses here is *kauchaomai*, which is often translated as "rejoice" or "glory in"; the New Living Translation renders it "be glad." But the base word of *kauchaomai* simply means "to boast." That kind of makes it even worse, doesn't it? As parents, we always admonish our kids not to boast, because boasting is always bad, right? And in walks James, unabashedly saying, "Hey, you should boast about this!"

What on earth is going on here?

What makes this dilemma even more interesting is that the *kauchaomai* is actually used rather often in the New Testament. Including the times James uses it, we find this word about thirty five times throughout the New Testament. In every other case, it was used by Paul, but of those thirty five times, in only seven of them is it used in a negative sense. Every other time, this boasting, being proud, is a good thing. How is this possible?

I like the way that Charles Tyree explains it. He says this passage, "acknowledges God's providential care of His people as they live out a life of faith in the wisdom of God. Such a life permits a legitimate form of pride…. While one form of pride is a sin to be avoided, the following expressions of pride are virtues to be developed."

In this passage, James addresses two kinds of pride that God's people should develop as virtues. Or, more precisely, two kinds of people whose circumstances each afford an opportunity for developing and displaying Godly pride: the rich and the poor.

Poor: Be Proud of Your Wealth

He starts out by addressing the poor, which makes sense, considering most of his audience would have fallen into this category; remember that the Christian Jews James is writing to were the poorest of the poor, rejected by everyone around them and thus, often quite destitute in their circumstances.

To these believers, people who were experiencing poverty like we probably can't even imagine, James says, **"take pride in [your] high position."** I don't know about you, but to me that seems like rather an odd thing to say, particularly considering the fact that the word he uses to identify them, translated here as **of humble means**, literally means "lowly." What high position was James thinking of here? Apparently he felt his meaning was completely obvious because he just leaves it at that: those who are lowly should rejoice in their high position. Clearly in his mind, no further explanation was necessary.

But when you put this comment into the larger context of the first chapter of this epistle, I would suggest that the meaning is fairly clear. The overall message James wants to communicate in this chapter comes in verse two: **consider it nothing but joy when you fall into all sorts of trials**, because, as we've already discovered, trials produce perseverance and perseverance produces mature faith.

A common belief among the Jews of the first century was that poverty was always connected to sin. Various passages in Proverbs and the prophets seem to indicate this connection, and the prosperity of the Patriarchs and kings like Solomon and David, who were considered righteous, served to reinforce this idea. So the prevailing wisdom of the day was that material wealth and prosperity were signs of God's favor and poverty was equally a sign of God's wrath. So when the Jews saw someone living in poverty, their first thought was, "What sin did this person commit that caused God to punish them with poverty?"

James is clearly indicating that the poverty the people of his audience suffered under was not a punishment but rather a privilege; it was an opportunity from God to learn perseverance and to become more mature in their faith. At the same time, it would seem that James is seeking to give these impoverished believers an eternal perspective on their situation. When your eyes are on this world, material possessions, or the lack of them, become one of the primary focuses of your life; when that is your focus, poverty becomes a very real humiliation, a clear, undeniable sign of failure. James wants to remind these believers of their true position from God's perspective: each one of them is a "child of God," a member of the royal priesthood, one whose name is written in God's Book of Life! And not only all that, they are also heirs of the eternal riches of Christ; all of the limitless wealth of Heaven will one day be theirs. Though the world disdains them and considers them lowly, in truth they hold the highest position possible: they are servants of Christ.

And that, according to James, is something worth being proud of.

Rich: Be Proud of Your Lowliness

Then, James turns his attention to the rich, but once again, his comments to them are not what I would have expected. If the poor, the lowly have cause to rejoice in their high position in Christ, wouldn't the rich, who have material wealth as well, have all the more reason for such pride? But instead, James tells the rich believer that their pride, **"should be in his humiliation."**

And I just love the reason James gives to justify this conclusion: Your pride should be in your poverty, **"because [you] will pass away like a wildflower in the meadow."**

Many commentators mentioned that this image of wildflowers was very expressive to the Jews of the first century. During certain seasons in Israel, if it rains during the night, by morning thousands of new flowers will have sprung up, covering the hills and fields with amazing color and beauty. But as soon as the afternoon sun comes out, they wither and fade away. So this visual image James uses was one that the Jews would clearly and immediately understand: the material blessings of this world that set you apart, that make you beautiful, are a thing of the moment; when the sun comes up, they will vanish. Isn't that an encouraging thought?

But in one sense, it actually is an encouragement. That material riches will fade away is a fact that no one can deny; either fortune will turn and one who was prosperous will fall into poverty, or you will leave your wealth behind in death. But one way or another, the rich man's wealth will not last forever. And if material riches are all the wealth you have, then in the long run, you really don't have much. As the Believer's Bible Commentary puts it, "If a man has nothing but material wealth, then all his plans will end at the grave,"[18] if not before. The believer's treasure, however, is found in Heaven and it is treasure that will never be lost or fade away. Just as the poor believers are exalted because of their spiritual wealth, those who are materially rich can also take pride in their wealth in Christ, wealth that they will never loose.

But, just as he did with the poor, I think James is also encouraging these rich believers to maintain a Godly perspective. Jesus made it clear that much will be required of anyone who has been given much. Those whom God has made wealthy here on earth have a responsibility to use that wealth in the service of God's Kingdom. So, Tyree suggests that the low position of rich believers that James refers to here is their status as servant of all. Whatever we have in this world, that is what God has made us stewards of, and He expects us to use all that He has given us in His service. As Tyree puts it, "To take pride in wealth that is given by God is to pretend that human effort produced it. But to humbly accept the role of a manager serving the interests of the Kingdom of God with every resource He has given gives glory to our Heavenly Provider."

One who understands where their true wealth lies, and one who recognizes their role as a steward of what God has given them here in this world, such a one can, indeed, take pride in their lowly position.

Our True Wealth is Jesus

Ultimately, there are two general ideas that I'd like to leave you with as we close out this chapter. First, I think it is important to note that James is not really focusing on the relative wealth of the believers he is addressing in these verses. In other words, it doesn't really matter if you are rich or poor; what matters is how you live. Are you using the resources God has given you, be they plentiful or scarce, for His glory? Are you willing to accept whatever circumstances God puts you in during your time here on earth, be it living in plenty or living in want? Is your focus on what you have (or what you wish you had) now, or on the eternal treasures that God has promised to all who are adopted into His family through Jesus Christ?

These are the questions that matter. I really like the way Tyree puts this idea. In his conclusion, he says:

> Are you in humble circumstances? … don't waste time in
> envy of those with more. Rather than self-pity, exercise
> pride in the grace of God that has given you your position
> as a servant of the Lord of lords and the King of kings….
> Are you rich in talent or beauty or material success?...
> Humbly admit that these things are yours to manage and
> multiply for the kingdom of God for the short duration of
> this lifetime. Accept your added responsibility before God
> with the humble acknowledgement that you will need His
> grace and help to use these resources to bring others to
> know God's love in Christ.

And his final conclusion is this: "Bring glory to God and give meaning to your life by your attitude toward the material blessings your Provider has given you."

That, I think, really sums up the heart of what James is getting at in these verses. No matter what you have, focus your heart on God and take pride in your position as His child, using all you have for His service.

The second thing that strikes me about this passage is a bit more specific, and relates more directly to those of you who are working cross-culturally in full time Christian ministry. We missionaries, who are from the West but who are working in third world countries overseas, are in a rather unique situation. James talk to the poor and the rich as two separate groups, which normally they are. But in some ways, we missionaries really fit into both of these categories. When my family returns to the United States, it is fairly clear that we do not qualify as rich. We frequent the second hand clothes stores, we shop at the discount supermarkets, we scrimp and save every penny, because there aren't that many pennies to go around! So in that sense, when James encourages the poor to take pride in their high estate, he is talking to us. Our treasure is in Heaven, not here on earth, and that is something we can be encouraged by.

But when we are in Cameroon, there is a sense that we are fairly rich as well. In the missionary community as a whole, generally our houses are much nicer than the houses of the people who live around us. We have cars; our neighbors generally don't. We have utilities, like power and running water, that many of our neighbors don't. I think we generally eat much more expensive food than most of those who surround us. I could go on, but I think you get the idea: comparatively speaking, we have a lot; we're pretty rich. And I think it is important to realize that James' admonition and encouragement to the rich applies to us equally well. Our material wealth is very fleeting, because, if nothing else, furlough is coming at some point! And we have to be very careful that we keep our trust firmly in the One who gave us all that we have, rather than focusing on what He has given us, or (even worse) focusing on what we wish He would hurry up and give us! We must never forget that we are His stewards and all we have has been given us for His service, in any way that He leads us.

So no matter what your circumstances might be today, I would encourage you to follow the advice James gives us in this passage. Instead of trusting in the comforts and luxuries that we have, or lamenting all the things we don't have, rather let us take pride in our high estate as stewards of the King of kings. We are His servants, His adopted sons and daughters, and the treasure that awaits us will not wither and fade with the inevitable coming of the sun; it will last for all eternity.

Chapter Five: Temptations

James 1: 12 – 15

> **Happy is the one who endures testing, because when he has proven to be genuine, he will receive the crown of life that God promised to those who love him. Let no one say when he is tempted, "I am tempted by God," for God cannot be tempted by evil, and he himself tempts no one. But each one is tempted when he is lured and enticed by his own desires. Then when desire conceives, it gives birth to sin, and when sin is full grown, it gives birth to death.**

Periodically, the school where I teach here in Cameroon[19] holds a movie night, where everyone comes together in the auditorium in the evening and we show a fun movie. Some years ago, we showed the movie *Inkheart*. In case you are not familiar with that movie (or with the book that the movie is based on), it is about a man who is a Silvertongue, which means he has the ability to draw characters and objects out of books into reality just by reading the book aloud. Being a writer, I thought that was rather a unique idea, and it is an interesting movie (though I have to say, the book is better!). But what interests me today is one particular scene in which one character, who is something of a villain, confronts the author who wrote him. The author feels like he knows exactly what the character will do because, as he essentially says, "I wrote you that way." And the character takes great exception to this idea. He responds hotly, "You don't control me!"

I find this exchange interesting because in certain circumstances, that sentiment really resonates with today's Western mindset. We don't like the suggestion that who we are or what we can do is determined by someone other than ourselves. We don't want anyone to be able to control us. I think this is particularly true in circumstances where we are told we can't do something that we want to do.

But what is interesting is that there are other circumstances where we insist on the fact that we're not in control of our character or our situation, that we can't help being who we are or doing what we did. These would be the situations where we have messed up, made some kind of mistake or are being blamed for something. In such circumstances, our first reaction is usually to shift the blame to someone else, to prove that we're not really responsible, that whatever happened was really someone else's fault.

This Blame Game, as Charles Tyree calls it, has become rather enshrined in the wisdom and thinking of the modern world. We've probably all heard reports of criminals who place the blame for their crimes on their parents (or their lack of parents), their economic situation (be it affluent or impoverished) or simply on difficult circumstances in their lives. One flagrant example of this from recent history is the tragic shootings at Fort Hood in Texas back in 2009. You'll remember that, on November 5th, a Muslim soldier named Nidal Malik Hasan who was stationed at Fort Hood walked into the infirmary and opened fire, killing thirteen other soldiers before he was subdued. And, even though he has clearly, repeatedly expressed his sympathies with Muslim terrorist groups and has known ties to at least two terrorist leaders, it has been seriously suggested that the main reason this crime was committed was that Hasan had been ridiculed by other soldiers for his Muslim faith. In other words, it wasn't his fault that he murdered thirteen fellow soldiers in cold blood; he couldn't help it because people had teased him.

Of course, the Blame Game is as old as human sin itself. When God confronted Adam and Eve in the Garden after the very first sin, Adam's immediate response was, "The woman that you gave me made me eat it!" And, not to be outdone, Eve jumped in with, "No, the serpent made me do it!" When we sin, our natural instinct seems to be to do anything we can to make it someone else's fault.

One thing that I find very interesting is that the first person to ever be blamed for causing someone to sin is God Himself. Adam says, "The woman that *you* gave me…." The implication, of course, is something like, "If You hadn't gone and made that woman, everything would have been fine. But You made her, and now look at the mess I'm in!" Adam's instinctive reaction was to try to make his sin God's fault.

And that instinct, that tendency was, apparently, something that James had run into as he was writing his epistle, because, as you can see in the verses printed above (Chapter 1:12 – 15), he deals with exactly this issue.

God Is Not a Tempter

Notice that James begins this section, in verse 13, by categorically and unequivocally establishing the primary fact: God does not tempt us to sin. Period.

But that verse immediately raises a question in my mind: how can James be so sure that God does not tempt us? I mean, go back to the Garden of Eden. If God hadn't planted the tree where Adam and Eve could get to it, there wouldn't have been any problem, right? Wasn't putting the forbidden fruit within reach allowing the possibility of temptation? Or, look at the Lord's Prayer. Jesus taught His disciples to pray, **"Do not lead us temptation."**[20] If God never tempts us, why would we need to ask Him not to tempt us?

Part of the answer comes from the context of the whole first chapter of this epistle. James has spent ten verses or so explaining how believers should joyfully persevere when they face trials and difficult circumstances. And the word he uses for trials in verse two is *peirasmos*. The trouble is, the word translated as "tempted" in verse 13 is *peirazo*, which is the verb form of *peirasmos*. In other words, James essentially uses the same word; they are both the Greek equivalent of "to tempt" or "temptation." Apparently, this word was used to refer to both external trials, difficult circumstances, as well as to internal temptations, inducements to sin. And there is a logical connection between those two concepts. Warren Wiersbe explains this connection fairly well; he suggests that when God allows us to face difficult circumstances, we basically have two choices: we can trust God and persevere or we can look to our own strength and seek a way out of the trial. When we look to our own strength, we are essentially questioning God's love or His power or His faithfulness to bring us through the trial. And when we start questioning God, Satan (with, of course, the help of our own sinful nature) is right there with us, suggesting a "better" way out of the trial. That "better" way is temptation, and when we take that way, we fall into sin.

So, the trials that God brings into our lives for our good, to help us become mature in our faith can, when we seek our own way out of them, become opportunities for temptation, which gives us the impression that God arranges trials in our lives to entice us into sin. But in those cases, it is not God tempting us to sin; it is our own sinful nature, seeking to fix our circumstances in our own strength, because we don't trust God to take care of us. So God brings us trials for our own good, that we might become mature and we sometimes turn those trials into temptations, because of our lack of faith. Albert Barnes summarizes this idea well when he says, "If there was nothing *in the corrupt human mind itself* leading to sin, there would be nothing in the Divine arrangement that would produce it."[21]

Another part of the answer to this dilemma comes from God's character. James tells us that God can not be tempted to sin, which makes sense, given who He is. To be liable to temptation, there must be something in your character that makes sin attractive, some evil desire that only sin can satisfy; some lack of power or wealth that sin promises to fulfill; some deficit of happiness that sin claims to remedy. These are the failings that lead human beings to sin; we want one, or all of those things and we mistakenly, foolishly believe that our sinful act will fulfill that desire. But God has none of these things; His desires are only good, all the time. There is no shadow of evil in Him, and there never can be; that is one of the few things that God can not do: He can not desire evil, for that would be against His very nature. He is all powerful and possesses all things; His resources are infinite and all He needs, He already has within Himself; and He is infinitely happy, all by Himself – even before He created mankind, He was completely, infinitely content with His own company.

So there is nothing in God that sin could grab hold of in order to tempt Him. And because God can not be tempted Himself, neither can He tempt us to sin. As Matthew Henry puts it, "He cannot be a promoter of what is repugnant to his nature."[22] Think of it this way. There is a movie called *Indecent Proposal* (which, I must quickly add, I have never seen); the basic storyline, based on the summary listed on the Internet Movie Database, goes like this. There is a young married couple facing serious financial difficulties and the husband is approached by a very rich older man. This rich man says, "I will fix all of your financial troubles if you let me have sex with your wife for one night." Now, I would not be tempted by such a proposal in the slightest. Having money would be great, but not at that price. To agree to such an arrangement would be totally against my character as a husband; it would be a violation of my marriage vows and, much more importantly, a violation of my love for my wife if I agreed to prostitute her in such a way. And that is how God feels about all sin; to lead His children into any sin would be a violation of His nature as a Father; it would be a violation of His promises to us, which would make Him a liar; and it would be a violation of His infinite love for us as His children.

He just wouldn't do it; that's just not who He is!

Where Temptation Does Come From

But James doesn't leave the point there; he goes on in verses 14 and 15 to explain where temptation does come from, as well as pointing out where it leads. First, he makes it clear: God doesn't tempt us – we do it ourselves. He tells us a person is tempted, **"when he is lured and enticed by his own desires."**

There are three very interesting words used in this verse. First, the word translated as "desires" means "craving, longing, desire for what is forbidden, lust." In the New Testament, this word is used exclusively to refer to evil desires. Then, there is the word translated as "lured," which is actually a hunting and fishing term; it refers to drawing or luring game out of hiding with some kind of bait. And finally, the word translated as "enticed" means "to be caught by bait or entrapped." Another hunting term, this word was also metaphorically applied to immoral women who led men astray.

So the picture James paints for us is this: temptation comes when our desire for what we do not have or ought not to have becomes the bait that lures us out of hiding and ensnares us. Note that, in this picture, temptation begins and ends with us. It is our desires that set and bait the hook and it is our pursuit of those desires that makes us bite.

Then, James finishes this passage by tracing the consequences of temptation, illustrating, as Tyree calls it, the life-cycle of sin. Temptation begins with our desires luring us out and entrapping us. In the movie *The Karate Kid, Part 2* (from 1986, not the newer version), Mr. Miyagi tells Daniel that the best way to defend against a punch is "to no be there." The same is true for avoiding a trap; the best way not to get trapped is to no be there! So, the best way to avoid sin is to stop it before we are enticed. This means taking our thoughts captive and guarding our hearts and minds, filling our thoughts with what is true, noble, right, pure, lovely, admirable, excellent and praiseworthy.[23] In that way, we can disarm the trap of temptation before we are lured into it. When we indulge those thoughts, when we dwell on our sinful desires and allow ourselves to think about what we don't, or shouldn't have, *that* is when we begin to be tempted.

In his famous novel *1984*, George Orwell wrote about a language people were inventing called Newspeak. Newspeak was a language that was decreasing in words. The idea was to eliminate words for concepts like crime and disloyalty, so that eventually, people would not be able to commit any crimes, because they would have no words to use in thinking about committing crimes. And that is the way out in this step of the life-cycle of sin: if you don't think about it, chances are you won't do it. If you don't follow your desires, they can't lure you into a trap, and the temptation is stopped before it even has a chance to begin.

The second step in this life-cycle of sin, James tells us, is when our desire conceives and gives birth to sin. Things in this step are more serious. Your desires have led you into the trap, into a place where you have acted on them (which is, of course, what happens when you dwell on your desires – eventually, you will act on them), and that action was sin. At this point, there is only one thing that can be done, and here, I think, is where the metaphor of childbirth that James uses becomes quite appropriate. Once conception has taken place, there is only one way to end an unwanted pregnancy: that is, to kill the fetus – to have an abortion. In the same way, averting the birth of sin requires a death: the death of Christ on the cross. Because Christ died, we can seek forgiveness, even after we have fallen into sin. And He is faithful to forgive us, whenever we ask.

It is important to note, however, that this does not mean we will not face consequences. Sin always has consequences, and though at times God chooses to shield us from them, often we still have to bear them, even though Christ forgives us.

Just as physical birth often leaves permanent marks on the mother, the birth of sin leaves scars. But scars are better than the alternative, which is that, once sin has grown up, it gives birth to death. When we consistently and habitually choose sin in our lives, we become spiritually dead. Now, I realize I'm getting dangerously close to a sticky theological issue here, suggesting that James is telling believers that consistent sin in their lives can cause them to die spiritually, which, in the context of this verse, would mean losing their salvation. I don't intend to tackle that issue in this chapter (or in this book, or perhaps ever!). But James does make it fairly clear: sin is not a single act. It is a process, and the further we go in that process, the more serious the consequences become, until ultimately, the consequence is death. That is what sin creates: death.

Enduring Testing, Receiving a Crown

So James is doing more here than simply reiterating the truth that sin leads to spiritual death. He is pointing out the consequences of allowing sin in our lives and suggesting the ways that sin can be avoided before it ensnares us. And this makes sense, given the opening verse of this section: **Happy is the one who endures testing, because when he has proven to be genuine, he will receive the crown of life that God promised to those who love him.**

Now, if I had been writing this letter, I would have put verse 12 at the end of this section, because it is really the conclusion, the heart of the matter James is focusing on in these verses. Whether facing trials on the outside or temptations on the inside, enduring, standing firm, is the key. The one who trusts God and patiently waits for His timing when facing difficult circumstances and the one who trains their mind to cut off temptation before it has a chance to being, thus standing firm in righteousness, this is the one who will pass the test and receive the crown of life.

Now, I want to quickly point out that I have no idea what James means when he speaks of this crown of life. It seems fairly certain that he doesn't mean salvation, because he was writing to believers and he makes it very clear, in other places in this epistle, that he did not teach salvation by works. I like what the Believer's Bible Commentary has to say about this concept: " In heaven all cups will be full, but people will have different sized cups."[24] In other words, our works will not affect our salvation, our entrance into heaven. But as we grow in maturity, as we stand firm in our faith against external trials and internal temptations, we grow in our capacity to enjoy heaven. As C. S. Lewis puts it, we turn ourselves more and more into heavenly creatures.[25]

The Heart of the Matter

There is so much truth packed into these few verses, I feel like I'm only just barely scratching the surface of what's here. But if I go any deeper, this chapter might stretch on eternally, so it's probably wiser if I leave you with this final thought.

What is your opinion of sin? I realize most of us would quickly say, "I hate sin, I avoid it!" And I would probably say the same thing. But James points out two very real, very subtle dangers here. First, it is very easy to slip into playing the Blame Game. In fact, Western culture practically demands it of us. But when we give ourselves permission to blame our decisions and actions on others, we build a shield between us and responsibility; in essence, we give ourselves permission to do whatever we want, no matter how destructive, no matter how sinful. And, worst of all, we can do it with a clear conscience, because it's not our fault; we couldn't help it! When that kind of attitude becomes habitual, you are dead, utterly and completely enslaved by your sinful appetites while claiming complete innocence and righteousness. This passage from James shows us clearly where that blame game leads, as well as pointing out how wrong it is: temptation and sin come only from ourselves.

Second, James warns us here not to blame God for our sins. When we start to do that, it is possible for us to begin accepting the presence of sin in our lives. The thought process goes something like this. God is good and gives us good things. God tempted me to commit this sin. Therefore, this must not be sinful, otherwise God wouldn't have encouraged me to do it. That may sound farfetched to you, like something no one would ever be deceived into thinking. But I can tell you that I have seen many otherwise intelligent and clear thinking students doing exactly this. I've found them clearly violating one of the rules at RFIS and when I ask them, "Do you know this is against the rules?" they respond, "Yes, I know it, but last week, this other teacher let us do it, so we thought it was okay."

And that is what we sometimes do to God. We begin to imagine He has led us into a certain sin, so we embrace it, knowing it to be sin, as if it was His gift to us, instead of standing firm and rejecting it. And ultimately, that is the message I think we need to take away from this passage. God brings circumstances into our lives that we must learn to endure, and our sinful hearts encourage us to do things that we must resist. And as we stand firm in these areas, we begin to learn patience and endurance.

And we begin to become more and more the people that God wants us to be.

Chapter Six: God is Good

James 1: 16 – 18

> **Do not be led astray, my dear brothers and sisters. All**
> **generous giving and every perfect gift is from above,**
> **coming down from the Father of lights, with whom there is**
> **no variation or the slightest hint of change. By his**
> **sovereign plan he gave us birth through the message of**
> **truth, that we would be a kind of firstfruits of all he**
> **created.**

In the passage just before this one, which we discussed in the last chapter, James talks about the source of our temptations, making it clear that God is not to blame; rather, the blame for our temptation falls squarely on our own shoulders: we are tempted when we dwell on our sinful desires and are thus enticed. And he follows this up by highlighting the consequences of allowing ourselves to follow our sinful desires: ultimately, that pathway leads to death. Warren Wiersbe calls this the first barrier that God raises up to help keep us from sin: the judgment, wrath and eternal death that we face if we follow our lusts and allow ourselves to be drawn into sin.

Overall, I thought James did a pretty good job of highlighting the problem we have with sin, and emphasizing the vital importance of not following our sinful desires. But apparently he wasn't satisfied that his readers would be convinced by his arguments, because he spends the next three verses of chapter one (verses 16 – 18, printed above) continuing this theme. In these verses, James highlights two more barriers that God has raised up to keep us from our sin.

Do Not Be Led Astray!

The first thing that strikes me in this passage is how emphatic James is; he has spent the last four verses clearly describing how temptation can only come from us, from our own sinful desires and inclinations, never from God. And then he pauses to say, **"Do not be led astray."** Apparently, there is some danger that we will be led astray. You see, James understood the strength of our desire not to be responsible for our sin; he understood how much we would like to have someone else to blame when we sin. But, as the previous verses illustrate, indulging that desire means accepting as true a serious misunderstanding of who God is and of who we are in relation to Him. It means building a wall between our actions and our conscience, a wall that gives us permission to do whatever we want without feeling guilty for it, a wall that numbs us to the guilt and pain that would otherwise warn us that we are headed toward our death.

So James pauses to remind us: Don't be led astray! The word translated as "led astray" literally means "to roam" or "to wander." So basically James is warning us not to roam or wander away from this vital truth. I like the way Matthew Henry illustrates this verse; he says, "*do not wander*, that is, from the word of God, and the accounts of the standard of truth, the things which you have received from the Lord Jesus and by the direction of his Spirit."[26]

Every Good and Perfect Gift

But James doesn't stop with simply giving a warning; he goes on to describe, in even greater detail, the truth from which we should not wander. He tell us in verse 17, "**All generous giving and every perfect gift is from above, coming down from the Father of lights, with whom there is no variation or the slightest hint of change.**" Weirsbe calls this the second barrier that God has raised between us and sin, which is interesting, because it is the antithesis of the first barrier he identified. The first barrier is the threat of God's judgment: sin ultimately leads to death, so avoid sin if you want to live. This second barrier is the promise of God's goodness. In essence, it is an encouragement not to turn to sin to meet our needs, because God is all that we need.

Or, to look at it in a slightly different light, this second barrier speaks to our doubt. One of the greatest inducements that we have to sin is our doubt that God will truly provide for our needs. We forget how good He is, we forget how faithful He is, and, often because He doesn't act according to our time schedule, we begin to doubt that He will provide for us. So we start to plot and plan and seek ways to provide for ourselves, apart from Him. And thus, we fall into sin.

In the context of helping us avoid temptation, it makes perfect sense for James to remind his readers of who God is, because when we remember it, His goodness to us is a strong barrier that can protect us from the desire to sin.

And he packs too much into this one verse about who God is that it would be impossible to really do it justice in the space I have in this chapter. I do, however, want to point out two things. First, James clearly asserts that all good things come from God; he tells us, "**All generous giving and every perfect gift is from above**." One thing I find interesting is that, in the Greek, James actually uses two words for gift, so the way the King James Version renders this verse is much closer to the original: **Every good gift and every perfect gift**. The second word, the "perfect gift" is simply the generic word used for gifts, something given that is undeserved, not given in obligation or as recompense for anything, but simply a gift, like a Christmas present. And the word translated "perfect" literally means "to be complete." So the idea here is that God's gifts are totally undeserved and exactly, completely what we need.

However, the first word, the "good gift," is a bit different. It is, according to Strong's Greek Dictionary, a prolonged form of the verb that simply means "to give." Several commentators took this to imply that "good gifts" refers to God's act of continually giving; that out of His inexhaustible resources, He is continually giving us good things.

But I also think it important to recognize the implication in this clause: all good things come from God. Think, for a moment, about what that means. Do you have anything that is good in your life? Have you thanked God for it? Because it came from Him. Though we did nothing to deserve it, He richly blesses us with all the good things we have. I'm often struck by how little we acknowledge His goodness to us, how little we even recognize it as His goodness. I find this to be a very important reminder: God blesses us richly each day, and we ought to be more faithful, more deliberate in thanking and praising Him for the good gifts that He gives.

The second thing I want to point out is this. In the second half of verse 17, James waxes a bit poetical to illustrate another key aspect of God's character: God never changes. James says all good things come, as the NIV renders this verse, from **"the Father of the heavenly lights, who does not change like shifting shadows."** Maybe it is the English teacher in me that is so impressed with this, but I think this is an amazing illustration of this concept. James likens God to the sun, the source of all light in the solar system. And in this source of light, there is, as the King James puts it, "**no**

shadow of turning." What I find so compelling about this image is that, at first glance, it is a horrible illustration of James' point. Think about it; almost every idea or concept that we use to describe the sun implies movement or mutability. We say it is *rising* or *setting*; it *moves* across the sky, marking the hours of the day; it *goes* behind clouds or is *not shining* today; it can be *eclipsed*. All of these ideas suggest that the sun is constantly changing. But in every case, *the change is not in the sun*. Rather, it comes from a shift in our perception of the sun. The earth rotates away from the sun and we say, "The sun has set." Clouds move between us and the sun and we say, "The sun is not shining." Every time, the change lies with us; the sun itself remains always the same.

And that is exactly the idea that James is trying to communicate: God never changes. Those times when He seems so far away, those times when He turns a deaf ear to our prayers, those times when heaven seems empty and we feel ourselves to be so alone; in those times, the change is always in us, never in God. Because God never changes. And, in connection to the idea of temptation, this is such an important concept. The gods of the ancient world were, at best, unpredictable. One had no choice but to pray to them, because it was dangerous to ignore them. But gaining their attention was, in some ways, even more dangerous, because you never knew what they might do. They were capricious and would save or destroy on a whim. You never knew what they might do because they were inconsistent, and their gifts could be a blessing or a curse (though they were usually curses, if Greek mythology is any guide).

But the true God is always good, all the time. No matter what our circumstances, we can trust that He has not abandoned us and that His gifts are good. The best illustration of this that I know of is a story that a friend of ours, Margaret Dobson, once told me about Ruth Chapman. You remember, I mentioned the Chapmans back in Chapter Two: she and her husband Bob served with us for several years here in Cameroon; but some years before we met them, they had been on furlough in Canada when both their sons came down with malaria, and ultimately, both of their boys died.

Now, before this tragedy, everyone who met Ruth was struck by her unshakeable faith in God's goodness. Her motto was, "God is good, all the time!" Margaret was one of her close friends, and they would have long conversations exploring this concept of God's unchangeable goodness; Margaret confessed to me that her faith in God's goodness couldn't match

Ruth's, which is understandable; I don't know of anyone's that could. Then, that fateful tragedy struck; within an hour of each other, both of their boys died. Shortly after this terrible loss, Margaret called Ruth to try to comfort and console her. But toward the end of their conversation, Margaret said she just had to know. She said, "Ruth, I just have to ask. Is God *still* good?" Margaret could hear Ruth sobbing on the other end of the phone as she choked out the words, "All the time!" And it was that unshakeable faith in God's constant goodness that allowed the Chapmans not only to heal from their loss, but to return to Africa and continue their ministry for many more years.

The point is, no matter what our circumstances, we can confidently assert that God is good and His gifts are good, even when, *especially when*, those gifts lead us into times of trial or suffering. What a foothold sin would lose in us if we could just remember and truly believe in how good our God is!

The Firstfruits of Creation

Now, if this had been my letter, I probably would have quit there, but James goes on to mention a third barrier that God has placed between us and sin. That barrier is His nature living within us. James says that, **"By his sovereign plan [God] gave us birth through the message of truth, that we would be a kind of firstfruits of all he created."** Again, there is so much in this one verse that I know I can only just scratch the surface of it, but I want to focus on one word: firstfruits. To the Jews that James was writing to, the implications of this statement would have immediately been apparent, because of that particular word. It is the Greek word *aparche*, which is one word that was used to translate two different Hebrew words. The first meant "the chief or principle part," which implied the idea of the finest; the second meant "the first ripened fruit of the fields or the trees," which referred, in other words, to the first produce that could be harvested. Of course, this was a very important concept in the practice of the Mosaic Law. The Jew were required to offer to God the firstfruits of all they had; even their firstborn son had to be ceremonially presented to God in the Temple. Their sons, of course, were not sacrificed but the firstfruits of their produce, the best portion of their first harvest, was given to God in sacrifice.

There were two ideas behind this Mosiac concept of giving the firstruits. First, this offering represented the best that they had and second, it was given before God had provided anything else. So they offered the best in faith that God would provide them with what they needed. Now, James takes this concept, so familiar to his Jewish audience, and he twists it around. Instead of us offering to God, it is God who chose to offer us up as a kind of firstfruits of all He created. And the implications of this, I think, encompass both of the traditional understandings of the idea of firstfruits. We, as Christians, are lifted up in the world as an example of what God has offered to do for all mankind, if they will turn to Christ in faith. But also, we are lifted up as an example of what men and women might be, if they are reborn through Christ and begin living as God intended us to live. And of course, lest we begin to think too highly of ourselves, James makes it very clear that this honor has nothing to do with who we are or what we have done; we are lifted up because God chose to give us new life in Christ.

Now, you may be thinking that all of this is encouraging but not really very relevant to the idea of resisting temptation. How does all of this qualify as a third barrier between us and sin? The answer is, simply, that by God's choice, His Spirit lives in us. And in the same way that Spirit of Truth that He has placed within us makes us worthy to be called the firstfruits of His creation, so by the power of His life within us, we can stand against any temptation.

Wiersbe tells a wonderful story that illustrates this concept very well. He says that a boy in Sunday School was asked to explain how he resisted temptation. The boy answered, "Two men live in my heart: the old Adam and Jesus. When temptation knocks at the door, somebody has to answer. If I let Adam answer, I will sin, so I send Jesus to answer. He always wins!"

The Three Barriers

And that, I think, is what this whole idea that James is illustrating in these verses boils down to. As we rely on ourselves, as we seek to solve our problems in our own strength, as we doubt God's will or ability to supply our needs, as we mistake trials and suffering in our lives for evidence that God has abandoned us, then we give ourselves permission to blindly follow our lusts, which trap us into sin and lead us inexorably to death.

But God has raised three barriers to help protect us from our own sinful hearts. There is the promise of His judgment, that we might fear God and turn from sin. There is the promise of His goodness, that we might learn to trust in Him rather than in our own strength. And there is His Spirit, His life within us, that we might be transformed into the likeness of Christ.

Wiersbe finishes his commentary on this section of James with an excellent summary of our daily choices as we face temptation, and I think it fitting to close this chapter with his words: "God has erected these three barriers to keep us from sin. If we heed the barriers, we will win a crown. If we break through the barriers, we will find a coffin. Which will it be?"

Chapter Seven: The Righteous Life that God Desires

James 1: 19 – 21

> **Understand this, my dear brothers and sisters! Let every person be quick to listen, slow to speak, slow to anger. For human anger does not accomplish God's righteousness. So put away all filth and evil excess and humbly welcome the message implanted within you, which is able to save your souls.**

When I first gave the message on the passage we're looking at in this chapter, I opened with a short quiz that I'd found on the internet somewhere, a quiz that purported to be a test of people's stress levels. It was one of those quizzes which tries to trip people up by guiding their expectations so that they will give a wrong (and sometimes absurd) answer. For example, the one question asked people to say "silk" five times, then to spell it out: s-i-l-k. Then came the question: What do cows drink? And most people, unless they are paying close attention, will automatically respond, "milk," which is, of course, nonsense; cows drink water!

My personal favorite was the final question:

> Without using a calculator, answer the following question. You are driving a bus from London to Milford Haven in Wales. In London, 17 people get on the bus. In Reading, six people get off the bus and nine people get on. In Swindon, two people get off and four get on. In Cardiff, 11 people get off and 16 people get on. In Swansea, three people get off and five people get on. In Carmathen, six people get off and three get on. You then arrive at Milford Haven. What is the name of the bus driver?

This is a little easier to answer when you're reading it, but when just listening to it, you can understand why most people would immediately say, "The bus driver's name? We don't have enough information to answer that!" all the while forgetting that, at the start, it was made clear that *you* are driving the bus, making most people's answer an admission that they don't know their own name!

The point of all these questions was that sometimes, it is easy to hear without actually listening. And the connection between listening, hearing and speaking is a topic that has fascinated people for centuries. Solomon speaks on this many times. For example, in Proverbs 17:27 – 28, he tells us, "**The truly wise person restrains his words, and the one who stays calm is discerning. Even a fool who remains silent is considered wise, and the one who holds his tongue is deemed discerning**,"

Many others have weighed in on this subject down through the ages. Demosthenes said, "As a vessel is known by the sound, whether it be cracked or not, so men are proved by their speeches whether they be wise or foolish." Or Jonathan Swift, who said, "There is, indeed, no wild beast more to be dreaded than a communicative man having nothing to communicate." Or this anonymous saying: "It is a great misfortune, not to have sense enough to speak well, and judgment enough to speak little. I liked this one from Thomas Fuller: "Learn to hold thy tongue; five words cost Zacharias forty weeks of silence." Though my favorite, I think, comes from Mark Twain; he says, "It is better to keep silent and be thought a fool then to open your mouth and remove all doubt!"

There is practically no end to the opinions people have expressed on this subject over the years. And in the passage we are focusing on in this chapter (James 1:19 – 21, printed above), James also shares some thoughts on this idea, though, as I've come to except from the epistles, James has a rather different perspective on this topic than most of those I found.

Three Mature Choices

The first thing that strikes me about this passage is actually the first word that James uses, *hoste*, a word whose meaning is often rather obscured in modern English translations. It is often translated as "Understand this," as in the NET above, or as "Take note of this" (in the NIV); the King James (as well as some other older versions) render it "Therefore" or "Wherefore," which is somewhat closer to what the Greek word means, but still lacking a great deal.

The implication of the *hoste* is that the admonitions and advice that James gives in these verses must be taken in the context of what he has already taught us earlier in this chapter, a chapter which has, overall, been painting a picture of a mature Christian life: being patient in testing, whether from outside persecution or internal temptations, seeking wisdom from God and relying fully on the promise of His goodness to fulfill all our needs.

In light of this all-encompassing "therefore," Charles Tyree suggests that verse 19 outlines three righteous choices that mature Christians should make, choices "which can lead to the kind of holy life God desires for all of us."

The first of these choices is to be quick to listen. There are two implications that can be taken from this idea. First, we should be eager to listen to God's commands, and certainly, in the context of this chapter, that implication must have been in James' mind as he wrote these words. So much of what he teaches us in this chapter hinges on the idea that we are attending to, seeking out and actively following the will of God in our lives; the obvious extension is that when we hear God's word, directing our paths, we must be quick to listen. But this admonition can apply to all our relationships with other people as well. As Albert Barnes puts it, we should, "be more ready to hear than to speak; … we are to be disposed to learn always, and from any source. Our appropriate condition is rather that of learners than instructors."[27] I think I will wait until we get to chapter 3 of this epistle to explore the implications of this doctrine for those of us who are teachers by profession, but the basic idea, I think, is pretty clear: as a general rule, all of us have much more to learn than we have to teach; one mark of the mature Christian is that they are humble enough to realize how much they need the input and gifts of others and they are wise enough to know how much they need to hear and obey the leading of God's Spirit. They are, in short, quick to listen.

The second choice of a mature Christian is to be slow to speak. Now, in many ways this is simply the completion of the first choice, the natural consequence of being quick to listen, because it is virtually impossible to listen while you are speaking (the protestations of countless students in my class notwithstanding). But even more telling is the fact that, when someone does stand up to speak, unless they were compelled to do so (picture the student who is called on in class without raising their hand), the necessary implication is that they feel they have something to say. So it makes sense that someone who is constantly standing up to speak must think they have a great deal to say but not much need to hear.

Many television shows or movies, especially in the realm of science fiction, have one character who seems to know everything; they are the one who always figures out the solution to the problem, the one who is never wrong. And in most cases, this is also the most obnoxious character in the show, the one who is usually disliked by almost everyone else. Because their intelligence makes them arrogant, they communicate very clearly that they are more important, and thus more valuable, than anyone around them. And they certainly don't listen to others; why would you listen to someone else when you are the one with all the answers? Unfortunately, many Christians act just like that in terms of their spiritual life. Of course, they would never say it in so many words, but they give the impression, by their actions and attitudes, that they have nothing more to learn; they are as holy, as righteous, as they need to be and have no more need to grow. No more need to listen. Unfortunately, they also feel quite justified in speaking, often speaking condemnation or judgment on those around them who aren't quite as "spiritually advanced" as they feel themselves to be.

There is an interesting proverb that I wonder if James had in mind as he wrote this verse. It is Proverbs 10:19 – **When words abound, transgression is inevitable, but the one who restrains his words is wise.** Only the wisest of us fully understands how little we understand, and what little right we have to speak about anything.

The third choice a mature Christian makes is to be slow to become angry. And this is the point where I get a little bit troubled. The first two choices seem to flow naturally from one to the other: listen well, speak little. That makes sense. But James seems here to make a connection between speaking and becoming angry; at least grammatically, James indicates that getting angry is on the same level, connected in the same way as slow speech and quick listening. Of course, on one level, this makes sense. We've probably all seen someone on the street who has lost their temper; such a person almost always suddenly becomes quick to speak and slow to listen! But that doesn't seem to be the implication James is aiming for here. At least in my mind, this verse gives the impression that somehow slow speech inhibits, and quick speech encourages being quick to get angry.

There are two possible explanations for this dilemma, either of which I think is equally plausible. First, as Tyree explains, one who is quick to listen to God's Spirit has given God's Spirit control of their life, and that includes control of their tongue. As Tyree puts it, "A wise man allows the Holy Spirit to control both his tongue and his temper." When the Spirit is in control, you will not become angry unless that anger is justified, holy anger. The second explanation comes from Albert Barnes; he suggests that, on one level, this verse deals with anger in general: as a general rule we should be slow to lose our tempers and become angry. But more particularly, Barnes suggests that James is referring to how we receive the truth of God. When we listen to God's Spirit and His teaching to us is hard, when His Spirit convicts us of sin, then, in particular, we must be slow to speak in justification of our actions and slow to get angry at God, or at the messenger God sent.[28]

I rather like that idea, perhaps because the point Barnes makes is a lesson I know I need to learn better. When God convicts me of sin in my life or when He reveals how absolutely ignorant I am, I need to remember how important it is for me to be quick to hear what He has to teach me, how vital it is for me to be slow to speak in justifying my actions or ideas, and how critical it is for me to slow to get angry at the situation, no matter who God chose to speak through. Perhaps some of you struggle in a similar way.

The Fruit of Anger

Then, in verse 20, James seems to continue his thought to its logical conclusion: **For human anger does not accomplish God's righteousness**. This also makes perfect sense. In the context of verse 19, the anger we're talking about here is categorically not righteous anger, the kind of anger that is justifiably directed at sin or evil. No, we're talking about selfish and prideful anger, the anger of the two-year old who did not get their way. And that kind of selfish anger must, necessarily, lead us away from the ideal of the mature Christian life, away from the kind of life that God desires for all of His people, a life where we are working toward His righteousness.

So in that sense, this verse really speaks for itself. But there is one other, rather tangential point that I wanted to bring up. I call it tangential because, to be honest, I'm not really sure what to make of this. In verse 19, the word translated as "every person" is the rather generic Greek word *anthropos*, which meant "all people, all humanity." So, the admonition of verse 19 clearly applies to all people. But the word James uses in verse 20, translated in the NET as "human" is different. Here, James uses the strictly masculine word, the word that refers specifically to males, which means, at the very least, the NIV's rendering of this verse (**for man's anger does not...**) is closer to the original Greek than the translation given in the NET. Like I said, I don't know how much to read into this, but I think it is significant enough to mention; apparently there is something about a man's anger that James specifically wants to warn us about, that as men, our tendency toward anger *specifically* does not lead us toward righteousness. It is almost like James is saying, "When you get angry like a guy, that does not accomplish God's righteousness." Which is not to say, of course, that a woman's anger is necessarily any more inclined to righteousness. But it is worth remembering, men, that apparently we are particularly inclined to the kind of anger that moves us away from the life God intends and desires for us to have.

So Get Rid of Evil

Then, James moves on to verse 21, which is where I really started to have problems following his line of reasoning. In the first half, the message of the verse, the actual words James uses, are clear enough: get rid of or put away moral filth and prevalent evil. These words, according to some commentators, refer to something that is filthy and disgusting, something that is absolutely evil. Since the word translated "put away" generally applied to removing a garment, the image James was aiming at was likely of a shirt or some kind of robe that was covered in excrement, something that you would take off as soon as possible, without any hesitation or remorse. James uses the strongest possible terms to describe the repugnance of our sin to God, implying that this is how repugnant our sin should also be to us.

The second half of the verse seems equally clear on the surface: **humbly welcome the message implanted within you**. Most commentators saw an allusion here to Christ's parable of the sower. The Spirit plants God's Word in our hearts, both at the moment of salvation, when He plants the Word of the Gospel, and as Christ lives daily in our lives, seeking to cultivate the fruits of the spirit within us, seeking to make us more like Him. The basic message James is giving in this second half of the verse, then, is that we need to make sure the soil of our hearts is soft, ready to receive that Word, so that our lives might bear fruit.

As I said, on the surface, this verse seems to be fairly clear, outright saying pretty much what it means. But what about the connection? We have to deal with the connection of this verse to the rest of the passage because of the pesky "therefore" (translated as "So" in the NET) that James uses at the start of this verse. It is almost as if James was saying, "*Because* you should be quick to listen, slow to speak and slow to become angry, *because* man's anger does not accomplish God's righteousness, *therefore* put away all filth and evil excess and humbly welcome the message implanted within you, which is able to save your souls."

There are, undoubtedly, many connections you could make between these verses, many explanations of how these ideas fit together. But in my mind, it all hinges on one word: humble. I think Tyree explains what I'm talking about better than I can, so let me just quote him here:

> Humble acceptance rules out argument, resistance or refusal of God's voice. The pride that makes us deaf to what we cannot personally explain or understand completely is set aside. The anger that would interfere with God's message of love, that tends to plow up the good seed with the weeds, is humbly submitted to God's control. The weeds of moral filth and sin must be thoroughly removed. Christ is in control, producing in us a harvest of life and righteousness.

And that, I think, is what James is aiming at in this section: the life of a mature Christian, which is primarily characterized by humble acceptance of Christ's authority in their life, by a mind that is eager to hear the words of reproof and teaching that the Spirit gives, by a tongue and a temper that are wholly submitted to the leading of the Spirit, and by a heart that is soft and open to the Word of truth that Christ is planting there, so that there might be an abundant harvest of righteousness in every aspect of their life.

In other words, that we might be wise and mature enough to follow the Spirit's leading in all the choices we make, allowing us to begin living the righteous life that God desires.

James 1: 22 – 25

> **But be sure you live out the message and do not merely
> listen to it and so deceive yourselves. For if someone
> merely listens to the message and does not live it out, he is
> like someone who gazes at his own face in a mirror. For he
> gazes at himself and then goes out and immediately forgets
> what sort of person he was. But the one who peers into the
> perfect law of liberty and fixes his attention there, and
> does not become a forgetful listener but one who lives it
> out – he will be blessed in what he does.**

I want to open today's chapter with a quick discussion of cartoons, specifically two cartoon movies. The first is the classic Disney movie *Snow White and the Seven Dwarves*. As I'm sure most of you know, in this story there is a wicked queen who is obsessed with being "the fairest in the land." And, to help her in this quest, she has a magic mirror that she uses to keep tabs on her status; she constantly asks the mirror that now-famous question, "Mirror, mirror on the wall, who is the fairest of them all?" Everything is fine with this arrangement until one day when the mirror has the audacity to tell her the truth: "Sorry queen, but it ain't you. Snow White is fairer." And the queen, being a reasonable villain, immediately sets out to have Snow White murdered. Of course, if you know the story, you know that things don't turn out so well for her in the end.

The other movie I'm thinking of has a similar idea, and that is the movie *Shrek*. In Shrek, the evil prince is looking for a bride, and he also consults a magic mirror. He asks the mirror to show him the maiden he can rescue and then marry, and the mirror starts to give him a truthful answer, one that the prince doesn't particularly want to hear. But just at that moment, one of the prince's men holds up a small hand mirror and proceeds to smash it with his fist. After this display, the mirror quickly decides to tell the prince what the prince wants to hear, even though that message ultimately leads the prince into trouble.

At this point, many of you are likely wondering what these two movies have to do with our continuing study of the book of James. Well, they represent, I think, two possible reactions that people can have when confronted by the truth. And in the passage we're focusing on in this chapter (James 1: 22 – 25, printed above), James uses the metaphor of looking in the mirror to describe how various people react to being confronted by the truth in God's Word.

The Listener

James focuses on two types of people in this passage, people that he identifies as the Listener and the Doer. I want to spend some time examining each of these types of people, starting, as James does, with the Listener.

The first characteristic that James assigns to the Listener is superficiality; this person *merely* listens to God's Word. He is the man who looks in a mirror and immediately forgets what he looks like. Now, as I often do when analyzing a passage of Scripture, I started by examining the words James uses to describe this quality of superficiality, particularly the Greek words he uses for "merely listen" and "gazes." And I was rather surprised by what I discovered; I expected words that would denote superficial hearing and looking, one who listens with half an ear, one who simply glances. But those are not the words James uses. The word translated as "merely listen" is *akroates*, which means someone who pays attention to, who attends to and considers what has been said. And the word translated as "gazes" (which is the same word used in both verse 23 and verse 24) is *katanoeo*, which means "the action of the mind in apprehending certain facts about a thing; to consider."

In both cases, James is not describing someone who is missing the message of God's Word due to lack of attention. This person is not like one of my students whose attention in class wanders and who later discovers they missed something critical because they weren't listening. No, this person hears the Word clearly, they comprehend it, they get the message God is trying to share with them. The problem is, it never goes any further than that; like the Queen in *Snow White*, they accept the truth they are shown but refuse to allow that truth to change their hearts. Or, like the Prince in *Shrek*, they refuse to acknowledge any truth that might demand a change in their plans or attitudes.

To put it a bit less colorfully, the Listener is one who understands what God's Word is teaching them, but they never allow that understanding to shape who they are or what they do. Their understanding remains purely knowledge. They can discuss it, argue about it, write books defending their understanding of it. But it never touches who they are; they never allow the truth that they understand to transform their lives. So in that sense, their hearing of God's Word is superficial; they may have great understanding, but their hearts and lives are never touched by that understanding. It remains merely head-knowledge.

Which leads directly into the second characteristic that James assigns to the Listener: self-deception. The word James uses for "deceive" is *paralogizomai*, which literally means, "to reason falsely," and it was the word generally used to describe sophistry, a term in logic which is used to describe an argument that sounds plausible or reasonable but which is actually intentionally misleading or deceptive. And that, I think, is the implication that James is aiming for here: there is an element of intentionality in what the Listener does.

Think about the metaphor James uses. Imagine that you look into a mirror and see that your hair is messed up or that you have a smudge on your forehead or a large piece of breakfast clinging to your lip. For most people, it would take a tremendous act of will to see that imperfection in their appearance and walk away from the mirror without fixing it. If you don't believe me, try it sometime. I would be willing to bet that most of you can't do it; I certainly know that I can't! Once I'm made aware of something wrong with my appearance, my first reaction is to go and find a mirror. And that reaction is not so I can see how ridiculous I look; that's the unfortunate necessity involved, the part of the process that I would avoid if I could. Rather, I rush out to find a mirror so that I can fix the problem and stop looking ridiculous!

So, to put this into spiritual terms, what I hear James saying about the Listener is this. When we look into the mirror of God's Word, we see our imperfections, the ugliness of our sin, all the areas of our lives where we don't measure up to God's perfect standard. After seeing ourselves for what we really are, in all our wretchedness, it takes a conscious, deliberate act of will to turn away without allowing God's Word to change us, without allowing God to make us less wretched and more like Him.

If that still seems like a stretch, consider your own experience. How many times have you ever felt the conviction of the Holy Spirit, felt the Spirit telling you, in no uncertain terms, that a particular area of your life was wrong and that it needed to be changed? I would venture to say that all of us

have felt that kind of conviction at some point in our Christian walk. And
when you were in that place, I'll bet your first reaction was to resist, to make
excuses, to question if you were really hearing the Spirit, to put off changing.
By God's grace, sometimes we are able to see that reaction for what it is:
temptation, Satan's attempt to keep us bound to the chains of our sin. And,
recognizing our true situation, we are able to listen to the Spirit and be
changed, to be freed. But when we don't listen, when we succumb to that
temptation, I would venture to say that it is not because we misunderstood
what the Spirit was saying. It wasn't that we couldn't hear clearly or that we
didn't understand what He was calling us to do. I would venture to guess that
it was probably the exact opposite. We knew exactly what the Spirit was
calling us to do and we didn't want to do it! So we turned away from the
mirror and decided to forget what we had seen. We deceived ourselves and
allowed the truth we had heard or read to remain in our heads, without ever
effecting our hearts and lives.

This is the picture that James paints for us of the Listener. I don't
know about you, but for me, it is a picture that is painfully familiar, a picture
that I see reflected far too often in my own reaction to the conviction of the
word of truth found in Scripture. Because let's face it: change is hard!
Change requires us to admit that there is something wrong in our lives, that
we're not perfect, not just fine just the way we are. Change requires us to
give up those sinful habits, those sinful desires that we really don't want to
give up, because we secretly still love them. And perhaps most terrifying of
all, change requires us to acknowledge that God has the right to ask us to
change. Because if He is asking this of us today, who knows what He might
ask us to give up, to change, tomorrow!

Change is very hard. How much easier it is to simply turn away and
forget what we look like.

The Doer

Fortunately, James follows up this description of the Listener with the
contrasting image of the Doer. And here again, I am first drawn to the words
James uses. He describes the Doer as looking, just as the Listener did, but the
word he uses in verse 25 is different from the one he used to describe the
Listener. He tells us the Doer, **"peers into the perfect law of liberty and
fixes his attention there."** The word translated here as "peers" (the NIV
renders this **"looks intently"**) means "to bend forward in order to see more

clearly, to inspect carefully or curiously." The image is of someone who notices a blemish in their appearance when they look into the mirror and they stop, they bend forward to examine it closely, so that they can fix it, so that they can be certain they have utterly removed it. And this is a habitual action; the word translated as "fixes his attention" is *parameno*, which simply means "to continue doing something, to persist." The interesting thing about this word is that, in the Greek world of the first century, it was the word commonly used to describe someone abiding somewhere for an extended period of time. For example, Paul uses it in 1 Corinthians 16:6 when he talks to the Corinthian church about how long he plans to remain with them before moving on to his next destination.

So the idea that James is lifting up for us is someone who takes the time to examine themselves against the mirror of God's Word. This is not a casual glance to check their look as they rush out the door. No, they live there, they abide in front of that mirror. Just imagine a teenager getting ready for their first date. They may pretend they don't care how they look, particularly if it's a guy, but they will still spend plenty of time in front of that mirror, making sure everything looks just right, making sure there is no blemish, no problem that they've overlooked. If you happen to be waiting to get into the bathroom, it feels like they are abiding there, like they've set up camp and moved in for the night; they're not going anywhere for a long time!

Of course, if this was concern over physical appearance, this would not be laudable behavior (take note of that, any teenagers who might happen to be reading this!). But when applied to our spiritual condition, this is the kind of person James says we ought to be: the person who looks intently into the mirror of God's Word, the one who does not forget what they've seen there.

And that brings up the second characteristic of the Doer that James highlights here: they gaze intently into the mirror of God's Word, remembering what they see, and then they apply that truth to their lives. They do what the Word tells them to do.

And that neatly sums up the third reaction we can have when we are faced with truth. We can ignore it, refusing to acknowledge it like the Prince in *Shrek*. We can acknowledge it but refuse to change because of it, like the Queen in *Snow White*. Or we can accept it, embrace it and allow ourselves to be transformed by it. We can, as Charles Tyree puts it, "Listen to the Bible until [we] live it."

The Perfect Law of Liberty

And in one sense, that idea really sums up the point of this passage. There are two types of people: Listeners and Doers. One hears the truth and consciously chooses to ignore it. The other hears the truth and does it. And we, James says, ought to be like the Doer.

But there are two other points that I want to bring up before we finish with these verses. First of all, I was struck by the description James gives of what the Doer is looking so intently into: the perfect law of liberty. As always, I looked up the Greek for the three main words in this phrase. The first two, perfect and law, mean just what you would expect. In the Greek, "Law" refers to codes of conduct that are written down and imposed on people by the state; "perfect" means without flaw or complete, and it is a form of the same word that was used to describe when someone came of age, when the number of your years was complete. Used together, they imply the complete and flawless Word that God has given His people as a guide to teach them how they should live.

And then, there is the word "freedom." The word James uses here is *eleutheria*, which was actually a legal term that was used by the Greeks when they wanted to permanently and irrevocably free a slave. This was done through a legal fiction whereby the slave was deemed to have been purchased by a god; since the slave obviously couldn't pay for this purchase, his master would pay the required price into the treasury of the god's temple. This payment was given in the presence of the slave and then a document was drawn up denoting that the payment was "for freedom." After this ceremony, the slave was utterly free and, perhaps most importantly, could never be enslaved again because, according to the law, he belonged to a god. All of this was wrapped up in the word *eleutheria*.

Put these three terms together and you get something like this: "Scripture is the perfect, complete law that has been given to us by God and it contains the one way that we can be permanently freed from our slavery to sin." I would say that is something worth looking intently into, something worth dwelling in front of so that its truth can permeate our lives. So that we can be changed by it and thus be set free.

Secondly, I was struck by the outcome that James predicts for the Doer in these verses: **"he will be blessed in what he does."** Now, on one level, this phrase really speaks for itself, but I think it is worth taking a little time to walk through the logic that James lays out for us here. When we gaze intently into the Word of God, the only place where we can gain freedom from sin and when we allow that Word to speak truth not just to our heads, but to our hearts; when we allow what we see in God's Word to change us and we begin living as He instructs us, then, because we are obeying His law, we are blessed in what we do.

It is a simple, logical and inevitable progression. When you dwell in God's Word and allow Him to shape your heart into His likeness, you begin to live as He has called you to live. And blessing naturally follows. Now, does that mean that things will always be great and you'll sail through life with no worries or cares? Of course not; remember how James begins this letter? **Consider it nothing but joy when you fall into all sorts of trials** (in case you've forgotten). Trials and temptations and difficulties will inevitably come; they always come! But the promise God gives us here through James is this: No matter what our circumstances, no matter what we are facing in our lives right now, the best way to face it is to dwell in front of the mirror of His Word, letting the Word shape us until we begin to live it, until we start doing what it says. Then, as we react to those difficulties that we are facing, we will be living as God calls us to live, even in the midst of our difficulty. And we will be blessed.

As I was originally preparing this message, and as I've been working through it again in writing this, I was struck again and again by how important this truth is. It is so easy to slip into the habits of the Listener, going to church because it is expected but not really hearing what God is saying to you through the worship and the message, reading your Bible, even reading it daily, but never allowing what you read to reach your heart.

And please don't imagine I'm sitting here writing in a state of perfection pointing accusatory fingers at you! One of the most embarrassing moments I've endured as an Elder at the International Christian Church of Yaoundé, where these messages were originally given, was right after I had presented a message on a passage in Ephesians. In the message, I had listed five points that people could draw from the passage, five points that were a summary of and, in some ways, the main point of my message. After the service, someone came up and said they had tried to copy those five points down but had missed the third one; they wondered if I could repeat what it was. And I couldn't remember – to answer their question, I had to go back and look at my notes! So just because I'm the one writing all of this doesn't mean that I think I'm any better at this than you; I'm learning to always be a Doer as well!

This is such an important truth for us to learn, I think it would be wonderful to take a few minutes right now, wherever you are, just listening to what God might be speaking to you today. Take the time to really listen, to really dwell before Him. And when you hear His voice speaking to you, don't just listen. Go and do what He says, that you might be blessed in all that you do!

Chapter Nine: True Religion

**If someone thinks he is religious yet does not bridle his
tongue, and so deceives his heart, his religion is futile. Pure
and undefiled religion before God the Father is this: to
care for orphans and widows in their misfortune and to
keep oneself unstained by the world.**

Religion. That is a word you probably expect to hear about in church,
or in a commentary about a book of the Bible; it is also something that a lot
of people are talking about these days; various events in recent news have
brought the issue of religion to the forefront of many people's minds.

And it is a topic that people have talked about for a long time. As I
was preparing this message originally, I looked in my book of quotes[29] to
see what people have said about religion over the years; I found nine and a
half pages, hundreds of quotes, devoted to this topic. Let me share a few of
these that struck me as interesting. From George Bernard Shaw, we have,
"There is only one religion, though there are a hundred versions of it." Henry
Ward Beecher, an American pastor said, "Many would like religion as a sort
of lightning rod to their houses, to ward off, by and by, the bolts of divine
wrath." My favorite, though, was from John Newton, the author of the
famous song "Amazing Grace." He said, "The religion of some people is
constrained, like the cold bath when used, not for pleasure, but from necessity
for health, into which one goes with reluctance, and is glad when able to get
out."

But one place that speaks very little of religion, rather surprisingly, is
Scripture. The word is used only five times in the New Testament and not
once in the Old (at least in the King James and NIV translations). And there
are four different Greek words that are regularly translated as "religion" so
each of them is actually only used once or twice throughout Scripture. So
overall, the Bible doesn't have much to say about the concept of religion; it
has other, more important things to talk about, apparently. But two of those
five occurrences of the word "religion" happen in the next passage we come
to in our study of James: Chapter 1: 26 – 27 (printed above). So what does
James have to tell us about religion?

If You Seem to be Religious

Here again, James is laying out a contrast for us; in the preceding passage, which we talked about in the last chapter, he sets out a contrast between the Listener and the Doer; the one hears the message of God's Word but immediately forgets what it says and the other hears the same message but takes it to heart and does what it says to do. This second contrast centers around religion, and the first half of this contrast that James investigates is religion that is vain or worthless.

As always, the first thing that strikes me is the words that James uses. The NET translates the first phrase of verse 26 as, **"If someone thinks he is religious**...." The New Living Translation is similar: **"If you claim to be religious...."** But the King James Version has a slightly different phrasing, one which I think actually follows the original more closely; it says, **"If any man among you seem to be religious...."** In each case, the entire phrase hinges on that word "seem." And the Greek word used here refers to the idea of a person's reputation, describing the impression others have of someone as a result of their actions. And that's the key: *because of what they do*. They appear to be, they seem to be, their actions make the claim that they are this type of person. So James is referring here to people who, by virtue of their actions, have earned a reputation for being religious.

Now, think with me for a moment: What kind of actions would earn someone such a reputation? Going to church each week? Praying in public? Being asked to give the message in church? Serving as an elder of the church? Choosing to work in full time Christian ministry? Leaving your home culture to work overseas as a missionary? I wonder how many of you reading this today have, by virtue of your actions, earned a reputation for being religious?

That is the person James is describing for us, one who is doing things that people generally believe a religious person ought to do, and thus one who is considered to be religious. And James has just one criticism to level at this person: they do not keep a tight rein on their tongue. I like the way the King James translates this phrase: **"he bridleth not his tongue."** Because that is what the Greek word literally means: to lead by a bridle or, metaphorically, to restrain or hold in check.

Now, James elaborates on this metaphor significantly in Chapter 3 of his epistle, so I'm not going to go into it very deeply here, but the picture is

of someone who is on a horse but who has ceased to be a rider; they have lost
the ability to control the horse, which is what the bridle does, and so they
have become merely a passenger, going wherever the horse wants to take
them.

This is the basic picture that James paints for us in the first half of
verse 26: someone who is doing all these things that religious people ought to
do but who is unable or unwilling to control their tongue. And James uses
one word to sum up this person's religion. In the Greek, it is the word
matai ŏ s. Various English versions translate this as "vain" or "worthless" or,
as the NET does above, "futile." But its most common use in the first century
was to describe the empty, meaningless practice of worshipping idols.

Now, I don't know about you, but to me that seems rather harsh. I
mean, here's a guy who is doing a lot of things right. He's doing enough that
he's gotten a reputation, because of his actions, for being religious. And he's
got one problem: he can't (or won't) control his tongue. And James writes
off everything that he is doing as idolatry: vain and worthless. But you have
to remember how closely James is paralleling the teachings of his half-
brother Jesus, who had a fair bit to say on this topic of religion Himself. In
Matthew 15, the Pharisees were complaining that Jesus' disciples weren't
washing their hands before eating. And, just to be clear, they weren't
concerned about hygiene; they were worried about ritual. This was a
ceremonial washing that the disciples were skipping, a ceremony without
which, the Pharisees considered a person to be ceremonially unclean. In verse
11 of this chapter, Jesus responds to this criticism with, **"What defiles a
person is not what goes into the mouth; it is what comes out of the mouth
that defiles a person."** Then, later he elaborates on this for His disciples,
starting in verse 17: **"Don't you understand that whatever goes into the
mouth enters the stomach and then passes out into the sewer? But the
things that come out of the mouth come from the heart, and these things
defile a person. For out of the heart come evil ideas, murder, adultery,
sexual immorality, theft, false testimony, slander. These are the things
that defile a person; it is not eating with unwashed hands that defiles a
person."**

So the Pharisees were focused on ritual, on the visible religious act,
but Jesus was focused on the attitude, on the heart. And that, I think, is the
crux of what James is trying to say in this verse. These outward signs of
religion, good though they may be in and of themselves, are rendered

meaningless if an unbridled tongue reveals a heart that is clinging to sin. And I think this idea becomes even more clear when you put it into the context of the previous passage. In verses 22 – 25 of this chapter, James condemns the mere listener, the one who hears God's Word but does not do what it says. Here, he is condemning the mere doer, the one who does many religious things but whose inner life remains unchanged, as evidenced by the evil that comes out of their mouth.

Matthew Henry sums up this idea very clearly I think. He says,

> When we hear people ready to speak of the faults of others, or to censure them as holding scandalous errors, or to lessen the wisdom and piety of those about them, that they themselves may seem the wiser and better, this is a sign that they have but a vain religion. The man who has a detracting tongue cannot have a truly humble gracious heart. He who delights to injure his neighbour in vain pretends to love God; … There is such quick intercourse between the tongue and the heart that the one may be known by the other. On these accounts it is that the apostle has made an ungoverned tongue an undoubted certain proof of a vain religion.[30]

So James is painting a picture for us of the merely religious man, one who does many visibly religious things but whose heart is essentially unchanged. And thus, all his religion is rendered meaningless, in vain, on the same level as the person who spends all their religious energy and action worshiping an idol.

True Religion

But then, just as in the previous passage, James shows us the other side of the coin: religion that is pure, undefiled, faultless, lasting. And the contrast between the two is immediately apparent. Vain religion is primarily made up of visible actions, building a certain kind of reputation among other men. True religion focuses on God; James describes it as, **"religion before God the Father."** So right off the bat, we have moved out of the realm of man's approval; our reputation, what others think of us, is not the focus of true religion. Only God matters.

And that, I think, is the overarching principle that James is laying out here, because he follows up this statement with two visible religious actions. Pure religion, he tells us, is **to care for orphans and widows in their misfortune and to keep oneself unstained by the world**." These are both actions which could easily be counterfeited by one seeking to gain a reputation for being religious. In fact, the most famous religious hypocrites in Scripture, the Pharisees, were well known for doing both of these things. What is important here is not necessarily these particular actions. Which is, I hasten to add, not to minimize these actions either; it is important to care for the outcasts of society; it is important to keep ourselves pure and not allow the world to defile us. But, as many commentators rushed to point out, James is not trying to give us a definitive list or an absolute description. As Albert Barnes puts it, "The apostle does not say that this is the whole of religion, ... he mentions this as a specimen, or an instance of what [religion] will lead us to do."[31] So in one sense, James is giving us representative examples of what true religion looks like, to help us distinguish true religion from mere religiosity, as if he were saying, "These are the kinds of things that true religion does; these are the attitudes and the actions that the truly religious person displays."

But in another sense, I think you could say that these two examples really do encapsulate what it means to be truly religious. They represent, or summarize two basic attitudes that are central to true religion. First, care for orphans and widows. In Hebrew history, throughout the Old Testament and into the first century when James was writing, widows and orphans represented the lowest, most defenseless members of society. Because of the way Jewish society (and to a large extent, Greek and Roman society as well) was structured, they had no one to care for them, no one to protect them and no way to protect or care for themselves. They were utterly dependent on the mercy of those around them (remember the story of Ruth and Boaz; that's representative of the life a widow faced). And Scripture makes it clear that they had a special place in God's heart; he cares deeply for them and greatly desires that His people should take responsibility for them. So in the context of this passage, caring for widows and orphans is saying, in summary, that true religion shows itself in someone who cares about what God cares about, someone who loves and protects those who are dear to God's heart.

And what about keeping ourselves pure, unpolluted by the world? Well, isn't that really just a description of who God is? He is holy, separate from the world, and He is pure, undefiled and undefileable. So James, in essence, is calling us to be holy, just as God is holy. True religion encourages the one who practices it to be more like God.

When you express it like that, this verse seems to me to be a pretty good summary of what true religion is: to love what God loves and to be like God is. Or, as other New Testament writers put it, to take on the heart and mind of Christ.

How Do You Measure Up?

So James leaves us, again, with two contrasting images: vain religiosity and true religion. And it strikes me that this is not so much a description as it is a measuring stick, an invitation to measure our own faith, our own religion, against the standard that James raises. I suspect that many of you saw yourselves in the acts of religion that I listed earlier in this chapter, because we all do many of those things, as well as, I'm sure, several other religious activities that I didn't mention. I think it is probably fairly safe to say that most of you, at least outwardly, have a reputation for being religious (else, why would you be sitting here reading a commentary on the Book of James?!).

How many of you, I wonder, also suffer from an unbridled tongue. Though only God knows your heart, I suspect many of you, like me, find this to be a rather sobering idea. If we take Jesus' word as true (and I very much hope that you do!), then the best measure of what is in my heart is what comes out of my mouth. And the best measure of the worth of my religious activities, says James, is the control I have over my tongue. And I suspect this does not mean what I say when I'm on display, those times when I'm standing in front of the church as an elder, when I'm standing in front of my classroom at the Christian school where I teach, when I am addressing a group of our supporters as a missionary; those times, in other words, when I know people are watching me. No, I think James means all those other times: when the taxi cuts me off in Yaoundé traffic, almost hitting me in the process; when I'm angry and say the first thing that comes to my mind; when I'm tired or hungry or frustrated; *then*, in those times, would you see me most clearly by listening to the words I speak.

That's kind of depressing, isn't it. And that is why James gives us both of these pictures. The one, to show us where we are and the other, to show us where we are called to be: demonstrating our genuine faith through acts of practical love and practical holiness, living as Christ lived and loving as Christ loved. And I think it is important to note that this is not an either-or situation. I do not believe James is suggesting that our acts of genuine worship are somehow negated by one slip of the tongue. But at the same time, I think he is warning us not to become complacent. He is reminding us that all of our acts of religion are not a substitute for a heart that is wholly submitted to God's will.

We need to be continually testing ourselves against the standard that James gives us in these verses. How well do we control our tongue? What does our unguarded speech tell us about what is hiding in our hearts? Do we seek out and care for those that others have rejected? Do we love and care for those that God particularly loves? And do we consciously seek to keep ourselves pure, standing apart from the corruption of the world?

Do we keep ourselves holy?

That is the way we are called to live. And in the power of God's Spirit, that is how we should live, so that our religion might be pure, faultless and pleasing to God.

Chapter Ten: Favoritism

James 2: 1 – 13

My brothers and sisters, do not show prejudice if you possess faith in our glorious Lord Jesus Christ. For if someone comes into your assembly wearing a gold ring and fine clothing, and a poor person enters in filthy clothes, do you pay attention to the one who is finely dressed and say, 7 "You sit here in a good place," and to the poor person, "You stand over there," or "Sit on the floor"? If so, have you not made distinctions among yourselves and become judges with evil motives? Listen, my dear brothers and sisters! Did not God choose the poor in the world to be rich in faith and heirs of the kingdom that he promised to those who love him? But you have dishonored the poor! Are not the rich oppressing you and dragging you into the courts? Do they not blaspheme the good name of the one you belong to? But if you fulfill the royal law as expressed in this scripture, "You shall love your neighbor as yourself," you are doing well. But if you show prejudice, you are committing sin and are convicted by the law as violators. For the one who obeys the whole law but fails in one point has become guilty of all of it. For he who said, "Do not commit adultery," also said, "Do not murder." Now if you do not commit adultery but do commit murder, you have become a violator of the law. Speak and act as those who will be judged by a law that gives freedom. For judgment is merciless for the one who has shown no mercy. But mercy triumphs over judgment.

The passage that we are focusing on in this chapter is actually one of the main reasons that I originally began this series on the book of James. It is, in fact, the passage that first got me interested in this book. Because it really speaks to the geeks among us, doesn't it. Probably most of us, at one time or another, have felt left out, like we didn't belong to the right group; like we were being excluded when we desperately wanted to be included. And here, James is clearly saying that people who exclude others, people who show favoritism, are wrong!

I always liked that idea; it made me feel quite justified in the anger and bitterness that I felt toward those who I thought were showing favoritism against me when I was growing up. In fact, once I even tried to use this passage to convict some people that I thought really needed to be convicted on this subject. I was part of a group Bible study when I was in high school, but I wasn't part of the "in group." Four or five of the more popular kids were very close to the leader and his wife; they formed an inner circle within the larger Bible study group, and I was always really angry that they were so exclusive within that inner circle. And of course, I told myself very clearly that my anger was all about the fact that I didn't like that they were showing favoritism, just like James commanded them not to do; that I was offended by their sin. Of course, it might be possible that I was actually just angry at not being included in their group, but that is clearly beside the point.

At any rate, one week it was my turn to lead the study, and I decided I was going to put them in their place once and for all. So I led a study on this passage in James. And it was really frustrating as I went through this passage that clearly condemned them for their sinful behavior, because they didn't get it! They just sat there agreeing with me but not ever understanding that I was talking about them!

Looking back, I wonder if part of the problem might have been that my jealousy of them was as much, or more, at fault for the situation than their favoritism was. Or perhaps the fact that I had missed the real point James is trying to make here in this passage. Hopefully, I've learned a bit since then and together we can figure out what James is trying to say as we walk through this passage together!

The Shortsighted Usher

As we've seen him do in the last few passages we looked at, James lays out two contrasting illustrations in this passage, each one demonstrating a basic truth. The first, found in verses 1 – 7, is an illustration that many commentators have called "The Shortsighted Usher." Two men come into the assembly of believers and they are treated very differently.

But I want to pause here to briefly mention that the word James uses for "assembly" is the Greek word from which we get the word "synagogue."

Some commentators were content to note that this was further evidence that this letter was written quite early, before believers had a specific word to distinguish their Christian gatherings from the traditional, more strictly Jewish worship at the synagogue. But in my mind, this word conveys a much simpler message. James chooses an illustration that describes people's conduct and actions within the church, in the place of worship. And though I don't think James is trying to limit his teaching to things that happen on Sunday morning (or necessarily to economic differences either), I do think it significant that the illustration he chooses highlights behavior in the worship service, in the place that we gather to show our love and devotion to the Lord and one of the primary places where we sit in fellowship with other believers. Keep that context in mind as we continue through this illustration James lays out for us.

At any rate, two men come into the assembly. One of them is rich; he's wearing a gold ring, expensive jewelry and fancy clothes. This is a man of wealth, an important guy. The other is poor. As the King James puts it, he is wearing "vile clothing." He's a nobody and his clothes show it. The usher comes and escorts the rich man to the seat of honor up front. You can almost hear him gushing, "Oh yes, we've got a good seat for you here, right up front!" I always rather imagine that he has to push someone out of that seat so that this rich newcomer can sit down. Then, he goes back to the poor man and rather offhandedly (that's how I always hear it when I read this passage) says, "Oh, are you still here? Well, just stand there in the back. Or, if you want you can sit here on the floor at my feet." I think it is important to realize that sitting on the floor at someone's feet indicated a master-slave relationship. To sit on the floor was a position of dishonor, given only to the lowest person in the room or to someone for whom you wished to show contempt.

So that is the first illustration that James gives us, and it seems rather obvious that, in this picture, he is communicating the truth that he articulated in verse one: "**My brothers and sisters, do not show prejudice if you possess faith in our glorious Lord Jesus Christ.**" Overall, a fairly clear, straightforward statement. But the word "prejudice," often translated in modern versions as "favoritism" and which the King James translates as "respect of persons," that word is critical to understanding what James is trying to communicate here. The Greek word is the compound word *prosopolepsia*, which literally means "to lay hold of a face." The idea here is to be captivated by how someone looks or to judge someone entirely based on outward appearances. But what I find interesting is that this word is used only four times in Scripture. Three times, it refers to the fact that God does not play favorites, as, for example, in Romans 2:11: **"For there is no partiality with God."** The fourth time is here in James 2, as a command against showing favoritism ourselves. So the basic message in this first section seems fairly obvious: God doesn't show favoritism and we shouldn't either.

Warren Wiersbe takes this idea one step further. He believes that James is implicitly asking this question: How does the way we treat other people reveal what we believe about Christ? If we have accepted Christ as our Lord, then we should live as He lived. Did He judge others by outward appearance? Even the most cursory examination of His life is enough to show He did not. If we are showing favoritism against others when He clearly did not, what does that say about Christ's Lordship in our lives?

Even more chilling is Wiersbe's reminder that Christ Himself was despised and rejected because of His outward appearance. As Wiersbe puts it,

> The religious experts in Christ's day judged Him by their
> human standards, and they rejected Him. He came from the
> wrong city, Nazareth of Galilee. He was not a graduate of
> their accepted schools. He did not have the official
> approval of the people in power. He had no wealth. His
> followers were a nondescript mob and included publicans
> and sinners. Yet He was the very glory of God!

If we habitually judge others by outward appearances, if we play favorites, as respecters of persons, how would we have reacted to Christ? Would we too, have rejected the King of Glory?

The Royal Law

In the second section of this passage, verses 8 – 13, James is a bit less direct. In fact, he starts talking about the Law, and the image he paints here is one of a courtroom. The readers of his letter stand as the accused and Christ is the Judge, reading out the criteria on which they, and we, will be tried. Did you keep the royal law of love: Love your neighbor as yourself? If so, then you are innocent or, as James puts it, **"you are doing well."** Or, did you show favoritism? If so, then you are a lawbreaker, guilty of sin.

There are, undoubtedly, many lessons you could draw from these six verses; I just want to point out a few of them. First, James mentions the royal law of Scripture, the Law Christ highlights as the second most important: Love your neighbor as yourself. Many of the commentators I read focused on that word royal; how can this particular law be said to be royal? Wiersbe had two possible answers to that question. First, it was given by the King; God gave it as part of the law in Leviticus 19 and Jesus affirmed it in His teaching to the disciples. Second, it is royal because it rules all other laws. In terms of human interactions, if we all kept this one law, no other laws would be needed; Jesus says this is one of the two that sum up all the Law and the prophets.

Charles Tyree adds a few more answers to this question. According to John 13, the way we love others shows us to be disciples of Christ. First John 4 says that our love for others is one proof of our salvation. First Corinthians 13 teaches that love is the most enduring of the Fruits of the Spirit. And perhaps most tellingly, love is one of God's primary aspects; as 1 John 4:8 says, **"God is love."** So according to Scripture, loving others is rather important.

Not only is it the royal law, but also, when we obey it, verse eight of this chapter tells us that we **"are doing well."** The word translated "well" comes from a Greek word that denotes "that which is intrinsically good." Tyree points out that by phrasing this in the conditional (If you keep…), basically James is making verse eight a question: Do you keep the royal law of love? Do you love your neighbor as yourself?

The second thing that strikes me in this section is how serious James makes favoritism out to be. He says, **"But if you show prejudice, you are committing sin and are convicted by the law as violators."** So, showing partiality to certain people is a sin; seems pretty straightforward. But I think James uses the word "violators" here quite purposefully. I think he was speaking directly against a problem that was rampant in the Jewish culture of his day. Overall, the Jews were very place conscious. They all wanted to have the place of honor in their gatherings, to be respected and known as they went through their cities. And most of their quest for honor was centered around religious duty. They wanted to be known as the wisest rabbi, the one who knew all the Law. They wanted to be the one who prayed most fervently and most effectively. They wanted to be able to say they kept all the Law perfectly.

And just like any other place conscious culture, they actively looked down on those who were not as good as they were. The gentiles, who were not God's chosen people. The "sinners" who were not as close to God as they were. The Romans, who were enemies of God's people. There were all sorts of people they venerated, based on outward appearance, and many that they persecuted for the same reason.

And James is cutting at the heart of their pride in this section. He boldly proclaims, "When you show favoritism, when you honor some more than others because of externals, you break the Law that you claim to know and venerate and uphold. You become just like those that you reject as sinners."

Tyree suggests that the sins James uses as examples are actually an extension of this idea. Adultery and murder are generally considered two very serious sins (particularly so to the Jews of the first century), and it is a rather amusing picture to imagine a murderer standing before God's throne trying to justify his crimes with the defense, "But I was faithful to my wife!" But also important to remember is the fact that adultery is the metaphor that God frequently chooses in the Old Testament to describe the idolatry that Israel constantly fell into. So it is very possible that James is making a connection between the practice of favoritism and the sin of idolatry, as if to say that when you favor others, you are seeking after what they have (be that wealth, good looks, fame, or whatever). Is that not showing more regard for those things than for the image of God that is in all people? And showing that kind of regard for anyone or anything other than God is what idolatry means.

So James uses these two specific sins to further drive home his point: when you show favoritism, you become guilty of adultery, you become guilty of murder; you become guilty of breaking all the Law. Which brings up another point that is worth mentioning just briefly. James makes it clear that he does not view the Law of God as many disparate, unrelated rules. Rather, he sees the Law as a unified expression of God's will. The Law defines what God wants of His people. When you look at it that way, it becomes clear that you can't simply break any one single law while keeping all the others. They're all connected – they are all, together, God's will for our lives. And when we break God's will in one place, we've broken all of it. When we play favorites, we become lawbreakers.

And that brings us neatly to the final idea that I want to point out in this section: the emphasis that James puts on not treating others with partiality. We are told in verse twelve that we should, **"Speak and act as those who will be judged by a law that gives freedom."** Think about how comprehensive that is. Everything that we say, everything that we do ought to be governed by this royal law of love, the law which gives freedom. And God will hold us accountable for how well we measure up to that royal law. Tyree explains this concept very well. He says, "Believers are not saved by their obedience to the law, but they are going to be judged by it. An answer will be given to the King for the words we have said and the things we have done or not done in regard to our neighbors."

Those of us who have lived our lives abiding by this law, showing love for all those around us, will find freedom in that day of judgment, both freedom from guilt and freedom from God's displeasure. And it seems equally clear what will be found on that day by those of us who don't abide by this law.

Mercy Triumphs

So, in this section James gives us two illustrations, each one pointing to an important truth: we should not show partiality or judge others based on outward appearances; rather, we should live our lives governed by the royal law of love.

So where does all of this leave us? I ask this question in some frustration because, as I prepared this message, I found it difficult to pull together all the many different ideas and trains of thought that I find in this passage, fighting to weave them together into some kind of coherent point. If you've found yourself struggling to make sense of my logic throughout this chapter, that's probably proof enough that I haven't succeeded very well!

But fortunately, James closes this passage with what I think he means as a practical application for all of this. And that is simply, show mercy.

Mercy really is the summation of this entire passage. Mercy is showing love and kindness to those who don't deserve it. Mercy is serving and helping those who can't or won't repay us, or even thank us. Mercy is working for the good of those who are working for our ill.

That is what God has shown to us; while we were still sinners, He loved us and sent His Son to die for us, that we might be reconciled with Him. Not because we deserved it or because He somehow needed us, but simply because He loves us. When we, who have tasted such mercy, refuse to show mercy to those around us, God is very displeased. Remember the parable of the unmerciful servant in Matthew 18? God desires and expects us to show this kind of mercy to everyone around us, because we, above all other people, know what it means to be shown mercy.

And that, I think, is the point that I missed back when I was in high school. I saw this passage in James as a condemnation of behavior in others that I didn't like, and I wanted to use it as a bludgeon to strike them down. But never once did I consider how unmerciful, how judgmental my own thoughts and actions were. I never realized that James was calling me to love them, even though they had rejected me.

I hope that is the point you can take away from the rather jumbled message of this chapter. Maybe the picture of partiality between the rich and the poor man seems exaggerated to you; you're thinking, "I would never do something like that!" And I agree – most of us probably wouldn't. But where do we show partiality? What kinds of people, based on outward appearance, do we tend to show preference to? Who do we discriminate against?

I suspect the answers to these questions will be different for each of us, but they are questions worth asking, questions worth seeking honest answers to, because this is the standard that God is raising for us as believers. As long as we harbor discrimination against or favoritism for anyone, we are violating this standard. God calls us to live all our lives, in everything we say and do, by the law of love: loving others as we love ourselves. Even when, especially when, they don't deserve it.

My prayer for all of us today is that we might be men and women who uphold this royal law of love, that in all we do, in all we say, in all our interactions with others, in every aspect of our lives, the love of our Savior and Lord might shine clearly through.

Chapter Eleven: True Faith

James 2: 14 – 26

What good is it, my brothers and sisters, if someone claims to have faith but does not have works? Can this kind of faith save him? If a brother or sister is poorly clothed and lacks daily food, and one of you says to them, "Go in peace, keep warm and eat well," but you do not give them what the body needs, what good is it? So also faith, if it does not have works, is dead being by itself. But someone will say, "You have faith and I have works." Show me your faith without works and I will show you faith by my works. You believe that God is one; well and good. Even the demons believe that – and tremble with fear.

But would you like evidence, you empty fellow, that faith without works is useless? Was not Abraham our father justified by works when he offered Isaac his son on the altar? You see that his faith was working together with his works and his faith was perfected by works. And the scripture was fulfilled that says, "*Now Abraham believed God and it was counted to him for righteousness*," and he was called God's friend. You see that a person is justified by works and not by faith alone. And similarly, was not Rahab the prostitute also justified by works when she welcomed the messengers and sent them out by another way? For just as the body without the spirit is dead, so also faith without works is dead.

How many of you can tell the difference between a live person and a dead one? That's not usually a very hard distinction to make, unless you happen to be sitting in the middle of a lecture in my classroom, but even then, you've got a pretty good chance of getting it right. I read a news story some time ago about a woman who was approached by a homeless woman wanting a place to sleep; she agreed to let the woman sleep in her car for the night. Problem was, the next morning when she came down to go to work, she discovered that the homeless woman had died in her car during the night. She was afraid that she might get in some kind of trouble for this so, instead of going to the police, she covered the corpse with some blankets and left it in the car. Ten months later, police officers walking past her car noticed a smell;

they stopped to investigate and discovered the body, still in the woman's car. Yes, you read that correctly – *ten months later*! Obviously, just like Lucy, this woman had some 'splainin' to do! And it would have been a little absurd if she had tried to claim, "Hey, I didn't realize she was dead! I thought maybe she was just *really* tired!"

Because there is usually a fairly clear difference between life and death; it's generally not very hard to tell them apart, at least when you're talking about physical life or death. When you start thinking about spiritual life, however, the distinction becomes a bit more difficult, doesn't it? There is an old joke that Charles Tyree tells about a man who had a heart attack and died in the middle of a church service. The church called an ambulance and when the paramedics arrived, they carried out three rows of people before they found the dead man!

Okay, I know, that's a pretty corny joke. But it illustrates a significant point: it can be difficult to discern the spiritually living from those who are spiritually dead, and that is the issue that James addresses in the passage we're focusing on for this chapter.

But I think, as we begin, it is important to recognize that this passage is one of the most problematic sections in the book of James. In the first chapter of this commentary, I mentioned that this epistle almost didn't make it into the Canon; when the early church councils in the third and fourth centuries were determining which of the many letters and documents that they had were actually inspired by God and thus, should be officially included as Scripture, they almost rejected the book of James, primarily because of passages like this one, where he seems to contradict Paul's teaching on salvation by faith alone. Other church leaders throughout the ages have had similar problems with James as well, most notably the great Reformer Martin Luther. Luther pointed to James 2: 24 (**You see that a person is justified by works and not by faith alone**) as a direct contradiction of justification by faith alone. Because of that verse, he wanted to reject the authority and canonicity of the entire letter.

And make no mistake; taken by itself, that one verse does seem to be quite problematic; it does appear to be a direct contradiction to the doctrine of salvation by faith alone that Paul so forcefully and clearly advocates throughout most of his epistles. But in the context of the entire passage, as well as the context of the entire letter, a fairly different picture emerges, and I hope you'll stay with me long enough for us to piece together what that picture looks like!

The Three Faiths

Warren Wiersbe points out that James is highlighting and describing three different kinds of faith in these verses. The first of these is dead faith, described as the one who, **"claims to have faith but does not have works."** These are the people who, as Wiersbe puts it, "substitute works for deeds." They know all the right things, they talk a good talk, they can quote all the right verses and speak the language of faith fluently. But their talk doesn't translate into anything more than just talk. In other words, their faith is purely intellectual. They know everything they need to know in order to believe in Christ, but their knowledge never affects how they live their lives.

And the illustration James gives of this kind of faith is, I think, just priceless. A fellow believer comes into the church in desperate need; they have no food, they have insufficient clothing, they have nowhere to sleep. And the response they get, the help they receive, is merely words: **Go in peace, keep warm and eat well**! Is that not a perfect picture of pious uselessness? James follows this illustration up with the obvious question: What good did these mere words do for this person in need? How did their positive wishes meet the very real needs of this brother or sister in Christ?

But I think it is easy for us to miss the full impact of this illustration, because James is targeting one of the essential elements of the Christian experience in the first century church. Remember he is writing to Jewish Christians of the *diaspora*, the Jews who were followers of Christ living among the cities of the Gentiles throughout Europe and Asia. These people were, as we've discussed before, the ultimate outcasts, rejected by the Gentiles and by their fellow orthodox Jews. As a result, many of them were desperately poor. But in spite of their poverty, one of the marks of the early church, one of the things that set these first century Christians apart from the unbelieving world around them was their care for the physical needs of those around them.

They were commanded, from several different sources, to care for the needs of others. There was Christ's illustration of the sheep and the goats in Matthew 25 (**just as you [cared] for one of the least of these brothers or sisters of mine, you did it for me**), or the example of the Apostles in appointing deacons to care for the widows of Jerusalem, as recorded for us in Acts 6, as well as many commands throughout the various epistles, like Galatians 6:10 or 1 John 3:17 – 18.[32] In all these ways, the early church knew they had an obligation to demonstrate their love for one another by caring for everyone's physical needs, as much as they were able. So in this illustration, James is essentially saying that people with dead faith, with purely intellectual faith, have missed the most basic element of what it means to be a follower of Christ. They believe that wishing others well is just as good as feeding and clothing them. What kind of fool would believe that?

And the indictment that James levels against these people is just devastating. **Can this kind of faith save him?** Faith by itself, if it is not accompanied by action, is dead. So the basic idea James is aiming for here is that saving faith must necessarily result in a visibly changed life. As Christ taught in John 15, those who are connected to Him, the vine, will bear much fruit. I like the way Wirsbe illustrates this idea: "No man can come to Christ by faith and remain the same any more than he can come into contact with a 220-volt wire and remain the same."

There is no way around it: genuine, saving faith in Christ will show itself in good works. Therefore, faith that does not produce good works can not be real; it must be simply dead.

The second kind of faith that Wiersbe sees in this passage is demonic faith, which rather surprised me. Obviously, he is highlighting the shocking example that James gives in verse 19: **You believe that God is one; well and good. Even the demons believe that – and tremble with fear.** Many commentators pointed out that James is connecting with his readers' cultural heritage here. Traditionally, the Jews would affirm their continued faith each day by proclaiming a verse from Deuteronomy 6: **Listen, Israel: "The Lord is our God, the Lord is one!"** And James picks up on this in verse 19. It is as if he is saying, "So you believe that there is only one God? Great! That puts you on par with the demons!" Because the demons know very well that there is only one God; there are no atheists in Hell. And they even recognize the Lordship of Christ; almost every demonic encounter recorded for us in the Gospels involves the demons loudly acknowledging Christ's position as Messiah and the Son of God. So the demons know and believe essentially the same things that we believers do, but clearly that knowledge does not save them. This emphasizes once again, even more emphatically, that simply knowing the truth is not the same as having saving faith.

But what really struck me was the implication that Wiersbe pulls out of this verse. Dead faith, he says, touches only the mind; it is purely intellectual, simply head knowledge. These people know the truth, but they do nothing with it. But the faith of the demons is actually more complete; they know the truth intellectually, and they respond to that truth emotionally – they tremble with fear! So in that sense, the demons are actually one step further along, one step closer to true faith, than those believers who James is rebuking in this passage. Those who claim to have faith that is not demonstrated by their works are actually further from genuine faith than the demons of Hell, because at least the demons believe strongly enough to be terrified by their belief!

But I think it is important to recognize that we can also look at this truth from the other direction. One can know all the right things and be emotionally moved by that knowledge while still falling short of genuine faith, because faith that does not demonstrate itself in good works, even if it moves us emotionally, is still dead.

Pictures of Dynamic Faith

But of course, James does not leave us with only examples of faith that is dead; he also describes what Wiersbe calls dynamic faith: faith that is real, that results in a changed life. Rather than simply defining this kind of faith, James instead gives us two examples of dynamic faith from the history of Israel.

The first example is Abraham. Now, for the Jews who were originally reading this letter, highlighting Abraham as an example of living faith was a no brainer. This would have immediately resonated with the Jews, as I suspect it does for many of us today. And James points out two significant examples of Abraham's faith. First, he offered his son Isaac, the promised child of the covenant and his only son, whom he loved, on the altar as a sacrifice to God. And James explains that his willingness to sacrifice Isaac (in other words, his actions) proved the faith that he already had; it fulfilled the proclamation that God had made years earlier, when He first revealed to Abraham His plan, an encounter recorded for us in Genesis 15. God showed Abraham the stars and said, "That's how many descendents you will have." Even though he was old and his wife was old and they had no children, Abraham believed what God said. And, as Genesis 15:6 says, God, "**considered his response of faith as proof of genuine loyalty**," though I rather prefer the way the NIV translates this verse: God "**credited it to him as righteousness.**"

Note the connection that James is making here. God gave Abraham an impossible promise and Abraham believed. God saw his faith, his belief, and proclaimed, "Because you believe, I count you as righteous." And that faith demonstrated itself in a life of obedience to God's will, event to the point of being willing to offer his only son as a sacrifice, because God told him to.

And that's the critical point, I think. Abraham was declared righteous because of his belief; he didn't work to earn that righteousness, it was given to him, declared of him because he believed. But the fruit of his life bore witness to the existence of his faith; his faith showed itself in a changed life, a life of righteousness. So Abraham is a perfect example of the point James is trying to emphasize here: he was not saved by his works; rather, his works are the proof of his salvation.

But then we come to the second example James uses: Rahab. I like the way Wiersbe introduces this second example: "You could not find two more different persons! Abraham was a Jew; Rahab was a Gentile. Abraham was a godly man, but Rahab was a sinful woman, a harlot. Abraham was a friend of God, while Rahab belonged to the enemies of God." The Jews reading this letter in the first century would have been nodding in agreement as James spoke about Abraham's faith, but I imagine their jaws dropping in disbelief when James throws in, "**And similarly, was not Rahab....**" They must have exclaimed, "What are you talking about? How on earth can you put Abraham and Rahab in the same category?"

James can put these two vastly different people together simply because they had one important thing in common: they both demonstrated their faith in God by what they did.

There is one striking detail in Rahab's story that I want you to notice. In Joshua 2, she is speaking to the Hebrew spies that she has hidden on her rooftop. And twice in the space of three verses, she tells them that everyone in Jericho is terrified because of the Jews: **We are absolutely terrified of you, and all who live in the land are cringing before you.**[33] Now, in my mind, that can only mean one thing: everyone in Jericho believed in the God of the Israelites just as much as Rahab did. They had all heard the stories about the Exodus from Egypt and about their time in the wilderness and intellectually, they knew that the Jews were going to defeat them; they had no chance against a people whose God could do the things these Hebrew's God had done! And this knowledge touched their emotions: they were terrified! This sounds a lot like the demons James mentioned earlier, doesn't it! But only Rahab took the next step and translated her faith into action. And of the entire city of Jericho, only Rahab and her family was spared. Not only that, but her actions earned her a place in the Faith Hall of Fame listed in Hebrews 11!

In other words, Rahab is another perfect illustration of the point James is trying to make in this passage. Just knowing and being emotionally moved by your knowledge is not enough to save you; only if that knowledge and those emotions move you to act on your belief will your faith be proven real enough to save you.

The Faith of a Prostitute

Rahab, in some ways, is a very troubling figure to me. Have you ever contemplated the paradox that Rahab represents? She was a Gentile, a pagan, a Canaanite and a prostitute. She had no credentials that might have commended her. She had none of the teaching or revelation that the Israelites had about who God is. She had experienced none of the miraculous protection or provision that the Israelites had during their years in the wilderness. All she had were rumors of these Hebrews; rumors of the Red Sea crossing and the crossing of the Jordan River, and stories of their military successes against the neighboring kingdoms.

And yet, on the basis of only those rumors, she betrays her king, her countrymen and her gods. Without hesitation, she proclaims, **"the Lord your God is God in heaven above and on earth below!"**[34] and **"I know the Lord is handing this land over to you."**[35]

Where did this woman come from?

She had so little to justify her belief, yet she gave up everything on the basis of that faith. And even more significantly, she demonstrates a faith that is greater than pretty much anyone among the Israelites of the time. Not convinced of that? Then look again at Hebrews 11. There are only two individuals mentioned in the Faith Hall of Fame from the time of the Exodus: Moses and Rahab.

With almost no knowledge to back her up, somehow she got it right.

And that is what I find so troubling about her. I don't know about you, but I often find it hard not to look rather condescendingly on the Israelites at the time of the Exodus. I mean, they had all these miraculous signs, they had a physical representation of God's presence leading them every day, as well as His daily miraculous provision for them in the wilderness. For goodness sake, they heard the very voice of God at Mount Sinai with their own ears! How could they possibly have doubted God the way they repeatedly did? And of course, the unspoken implication behind that thought is, "If I had been there, I would've done better."

And then up comes Rahab. She had no good reason to believe, certainly none of the reasons that the Israelites had. And yet, she did believe, to the point that she was willing to give up everything on the basis of that belief. How many of you would be willing to do the same? Would you be willing to risk all that Rahab risked on information as flimsy as hers was? And God, though James, points to her as an example of the faith that we are called to have, faith that doesn't stop with our heads or even our hearts. Faith that moves us to act, regardless of the situation.

Over the years, God has used this passage, and Rahab in particular, to really convict me. I can't help but recognize how much more I know that she didn't. I mean, I've got the whole history of God's redemption laid out for me: the lives of the people of Israel, the teachings of the prophets, the example and teaching of Christ Himself, the teaching of the Apostles, the example of church history and the prophetic promise of Christ's triumphant return, the thoughts and writings of countless Godly men and women from the last 2000 years of history, not to mention the faithfulness God has regularly shown me in my own personal experience. Rahab had nothing compared to the knowledge of God that I have. But would I be able to do what she did? To give up everything to follow where my faith was leading me? And what does it say about my faith when I'm forced to answer, "Probably not."

Let me make this idea very specific. The place that this truth hits me the most is in the area of finances. As faith based missionaries, finances are always an issue for our family; all the income that we receive comes from individuals and churches that choose to support the work of Bible translation in Cameroon by supporting our ministry here; every month, people send money in to support out ministry and, whatever they send in, that's the money that we have to live on for that month. The problem is, we have struggled with low financial support for most of our time overseas (as of this writing, 23 years). We have often struggled to keep our account balance here in Cameroon positive, a struggle that we often failed in; sometimes for years at a time, we carried a negative balance in our branch account.

In fact, at one point, we had such a large negative balance, which had been negative for so long, that our administration got to the point that they said, "Because of this huge, longstanding debt, at the end of this school year we're going to have to send you back to the States indefinitely, until you are able to pay off the debt and raise more financial support" (and don't misunderstand, I'm not trying to paint our administrators in a negative light. They are Godly men and women who were looking out for our best interests and trying to help us work through a difficult situation in the best way possible). So, at that point in our ministry, in order to remain on the field, God was going to have to provide us with a significant amount of money, as well as taking care of a few other significant needs; in all, there were four huge needs that had to be provided, and all of them seemed quite impossible by human standards.

Then, shortly after our administrators gave us this ultimatum, God took care of two of those four needs, quite miraculously, even though, from our human perspective, that just wasn't possible. God did it anyway. And almost immediately after that, there was an afternoon when, as I was praying, I felt that God was very clearly telling me that we were not going to have to go on furlough that summer. The problem was, that just wasn't possible; our administration had already told us, "You are going to go on furlough this summer." The question wasn't if we would go; the question was how long would this furlough be. But God knew that our desire was to not go on furlough at that time, and I am convinced that He told me we would not have to go.

Yet, in the days that followed this revelation (and after He had already proved He was capable of doing the impossible), I found myself still hedging my bets. I was saying things like, "If we are going to be here next school year," or "If we don't go on furlough." And I found myself planning for the possibility that we would be on furlough, working on problems like trying to figure out where we would live and how we would handle schooling needs for our kids, practical details like that. Things you only really start worrying about when you know you are going on furlough.

Now, I have to emphasize that I fully believed that God had communicated this message to me; He had told me clearly, "You won't have to go." But in spite of that blatant assurance, my actions never changed. I acted as if His promise didn't matter, as if His promise couldn't change the reality of the situation, as if I didn't really believe He could keep us on the field. In other words, my faith never made it to my hands and feet; in the words of James, my faith was dead.

In a lot of ways, that was my Rahab moment. Everything logical or reasonable about the situation clearly told me to plan for a furlough; God was telling me to plan for the impossible. And, even with all of the assurances and knowledge at my disposal, my faith wasn't up to the challenge; it couldn't inspire me to act.

So the lesson that James is teaching in this passage is one that I am still learning, one that I need to continually test myself against: am I acting in faith based on what I know to be true, or am I holding back. Because, of course, in the end, we did not go on furlough that summer, just as God promised me. He provided everything we needed and were able to put off our furlough for a full school year, to a time when we felt it was better for our family to go back to the States. So, in spite of my lack of faith, God still proved Himself faithful; what a wonderful blessing to know that His faithfulness is not at all dependant on our worthiness!

I wonder if I'm the only one who struggles in this area. What is God asking of you right now? In what area of your life is He calling you to step out and act on your faith? Near the end of his commentary on this section of James, Wiersbe says, "Faith is not believing in spite of evidence; faith is obeying in spite of consequence."

That is the kind of believer that God, through James, is calling for us to be. Believers who are not content simply to know all the right answers, or content with an emotional experience. But rather, He is calling us to be believers who step out in faith every day, demonstrating God's presence in our hearts by the radical obedience of our lives.

Chapter Twelve: The Teacher and the Tongue

James 3: 1 – 12

> Not many of you should become teachers, my brothers and sisters, because you know that we will be judged more strictly. For we all stumble in many ways. If someone does not stumble in what he says, he is a perfect individual, able to control the entire body as well. And if we put bits into the mouths of horses to get them to obey us, then we guide their entire bodies. Look at ships too: Though they are so large and driven by harsh winds, they are steered by a tiny rudder wherever the pilot's inclination directs. So too the tongue is a small part of the body, yet it has great pretensions. Think how small a flame sets a huge forest ablaze. And the tongue is a fire! The tongue represents the world of wrongdoing among the parts of our bodies. It pollutes the entire body and sets fire to the course of human existence – and is set on fire by hell.
>
> For every kind of animal, bird, reptile, and sea creature is subdued and has been subdued by humankind. But no human being can subdue the tongue; it is a restless evil, full of deadly poison. With it we bless the Lord and Father, and with it we curse people made in God's image. From the same mouth come blessing and cursing. These things should not be so, my brothers and sisters. A spring does not pour out fresh water and bitter water from the same opening, does it? Can a fig tree produce olives, my brothers and sisters, or a vine produce figs? Neither can a salt water spring produce fresh water.

The passage we're looking at in this chapter is rather troubling for me, for several reasons. Most of all, it is troubling because I am a teacher by profession. I am also one of the acting elders for the International Christian Church of Yaoundé, making these verses doubly applicable to me. And if that wasn't enough, here I am taking the messages I have given as an elder at ICCY and publishing them as a commentary for you to read. So if James' admonition in verse one of this passage applies to anyone, it certainly applies to me!

But in addition to making me personally uncomfortable, verse one is also, as many commentators point out, a general warning that no one should lightly take on a position of leadership in the church, because such positions carry great responsibility. Church leaders will be held accountable before God for how they led God's church, and that is a weighty responsibility, indeed. Before stepping up to take that kind of leadership role, it is important to pause and precisely count the cost involved in becoming a shepherd of God's church.

To Be a Teacher

And the cost is fairly significant, according to verse one. As always, I like to look at the words that James uses, and in this case, two words jump out at me. The NET (as well as the NIV) translates them, **"judged more strictly,"** while the King James renders them as **"greater condemnation,"** which is a bit closer to the original Greek. The word "condemnation" is *krima*, which means, "the sentence pronounced, a verdict, a condemnation, the decision resulting from an investigation." So God is going to investigate our ministry as teachers; He is going to examine our teaching, our leadership of the church, and when He is finished His examination we will be judged accordingly.

And if that wasn't enough, James adds the word *meizon,* which is one of two words in the New Testament that is generally translated as "best." The other one, *protos*, means "qualitatively better," the first in rank or quality. *Meizon*, on the other hand, means "quantitatively better," greater, not in quality but in importance and value. So, in essence, James is saying that when those of us who presume to be teachers come before God's throne, He is going to closely examine our teaching, our leading of the church, and, because we are teachers, we are going to get more of whatever we've earned than other people will.

Now, I recognize that this brings up the somewhat sticky question of inequity in judgment. If everyone who claims Christ as their Lord is going to be saved, how can some people be more or less saved than others? That's kind of like being slightly pregnant or mostly dead. Unfortunately, I don't have the answer to that question (what does that say about my ability as a teacher?!). I don't know, and Scripture doesn't tell us, exactly what this is going to look like on Judgment Day. Believe me, I wish I did know; it has particular interest to me, given the fact that I'm going to be facing this, whatever it might be! But I do know that James clearly announces that teachers, leaders in the church, will face some kind of stricter judgment.

I want to be absolutely clear on this point, however: James is not trying to discourage people from exercising their gift of teaching. This verse is not a condemnation of those who would stand up and become leaders in the church, and I certainly do not want to discourage anyone who might be considering taking up that kind of leadership role in your local church body. But James is trying to suggest that such a ministry is not to be undertaken lightly, because we who teach from God's Word bear a great responsibility to get it right, lest we lead others astray.

The Power of the Tongue

Now, I realize that, up to this point, this chapter has been focused on addressing a rather small group of people; chances are there are only a few of you reading this who are considering, or who are even able to consider, standing up to become teachers or leaders in the church. I hope the rest of you are still reading, because there is more in this passage than simply a warning against casually taking up leadership in the church. As the King James Study Bible puts it, James' message here is twofold. First, teachers will face stricter judgment from God, and second, the primary tool that teachers use is the tongue[36], which is the focus of verses 2 – 11.

Obviously, James is continuing to address teachers throughout this section, but I think it would be rather foolish to imagine that he is addressing teachers exclusively. The principles about the tongue that James lays out may apply more specifically to teachers, but that certainly doesn't mean that these principles do not also apply to all Christians. Many passages throughout Scripture (not least of which is James 1:26, which we talked about back in Chapter Nine) make it quite clear that how we use our speech is a very important part of living the Christian life. In fact, Warren Wiersbe suggests that controlling the tongue is the third main characteristic of the mature Christian that James outlines in his epistle.

And starting in verse three, James lays out three pairs of metaphors describing the three great powers of the tongue. The first of these is the power to direct. James starts this section by describing how a powerful horse is controlled by a tiny bit in its mouth and how a large ship is steered by a small rudder. Both of these are relatively small items, compared to the whole, but they control where the whole animal or the whole vessel goes. The connection, of course, is fairly obvious: the tongue is a small part of the body but it has great power to direct your whole life, as well as great power to influence the lives of others.

Next, James illustrates the tongue's power to destroy, and the images he uses here are a fire and a wild animal. I found it rather amusing to read the more modern commentaries on this verse, because every one of them brought up the Great Chicago Fire of 1871. Though I have to admit, it is a very good illustration of what James means here. No one knows for certain, but most people believe that the Great Chicago Fire was started by a cow. Mrs. O'Leary, as the story goes, was in the barn milking her cow and the cow kicked over a lantern, setting the barn on fire. The fire spread rapidly and before it was finally put out three days later, it had destroyed three and a half square miles of the city, leaving one hundred thousand people homeless.

That's the kind of damage even a small fire can do. And in the same way, one small, thoughtless word can be devastatingly destructive to the lives of those around us.

The idea of a wild animal is similar. One of the questions I am often asked when we are back in the States is if I have ever been on a safari. Sadly, the answer is still no, even though I've been near several big game reserves; there is a large one in the Far North of Cameroon called Waza, and I've also traveled to Kenya, where there are many of these parks available. But I've never managed to actually take a safari in one of these parks, though I know many people who have. Those folks have told me that all over these parks, they have big signs posted, saying "DO NOT GET OUT OF YOUR CAR!" Seems like good advice to me; if you leave the protection of your car while in one of these parks, some of the animals there would tear you to pieces, because they are savagely destructive. But the idea James is aiming for in these verses is even stronger than that. He says look at all these powerful, savage animals. Mankind has managed to tame so many of the them, so that their strength is no longer a threat. But no one has ever managed to tame the tongue, because its power for destruction is so much greater!

Then, finally James highlights the tongue's power to delight. Now, both of the images in this section are a little bit different than the ones that have come before them, because James uses them to highlight what a tongue should be by illustrating what it shouldn't be. In the first century, particularly in the arid climate of Israel, most settlements were centered around a source of fresh water. The well or the spring or the fountain was one of the most important features of a village, because without it, the people of the village could not survive. In the first half of this pair of images, James raises a hypothetical situation. Suppose you were to go and draw water from the village well and, instead of fresh water, you got salt water. You were expecting water that would refresh you and quench your thirst but instead, you got water that was useless, water that made you thirstier. And his image of a tree is the same. Fruit trees were very valuable in the agrarian societies of the first century; they provided shade and were a reliable source of food. But it would be a bit disconcerting, to say the least, if one day when you went to gather figs you discovered the fig tree covered with olives!

Obviously, both of these images are a bit absurd, and that is exactly James' point. Our tongues can be a source of great encouragement and refreshment; we can bless God with our worship as well as being a blessing to others by speaking words of truth and encouragement. So how is it, James asks, that the same tongue which can praise God and be a delight to others, can also spew out curses and gossip and words of discouragement? His conclusion here is classic, though I like it better as the NIV translates it: **"Brothers, this should not be!"**

Controlling the Tongue

If you'll allow me to belabor the obvious for a moment, let me ask this. Why, exactly, should this not be? Well, first remember Christ's teaching about the tongue in Matthew 15:18. He said, **"the things that come out of the mouth come from the heart."** What comes out of your mouth is a good measure of what is residing in your heart. Which is why James, in verse two, confidently asserts that, **"If someone does not stumble in what he says, he is a perfect individual."** The Greek word translated as "perfect" in this verse is *telios*, which means "to be complete, or fully mature." In other words, when a believer is able to completely control their tongue, that is evidence that Christ completely controls their heart. Unfortunately, I fear the reverse is also true: anyone who is unable to control their tongue must be feeding it fuel from the fires of Hell that they are holding onto in their heart.

That's a rather sobering thought for me. If my words demonstrate how much of my heart I have given over to the control of Christ and how much is still ruled by my sinful nature, that's painful evidence that I've still got a fair bit of work to do in handing over to Christ complete control of my life!

But in practical terms, in these verses I see James setting up a standard by which we can measure our maturity in Christ. The more fully our hearts are given over to Christ, the more control we will have over our tongue, and the more fully our words are able to consistently be a blessing and encouragement to those around us. For those of you who, like me, may still have a bit of work to do in this area, I would encourage you to echo with me the prayer of Psalm 19:

May my words and my thoughts be acceptable in your sight, O Lord, my sheltering rock and my redeemer.

Chapter Thirteen: The Wisdom of Man and God

James 3: 13 – 18

> **Who is wise and understanding among you? By his good conduct he should show his works done in the gentleness that wisdom brings. But if you have bitter jealousy and selfishness in your hearts, do not boast and tell lies against the truth. Such wisdom does not come from above but is earthly, natural, demonic. For where there is jealousy and selfishness, there is disorder and every evil practice. But the wisdom from above is first pure, then peaceable, gentle, accommodating, full of mercy and good fruit, impartial, and not hypocritical. And the fruit that consists of righteousness is planted in peace among those who make peace.**

I'd like to start this chapter with a joke I heard a while ago.

A Software Engineer, a Hardware Engineer and a Departmental Manager were driving in a car on their way to a meeting in Switzerland. They were driving down a steep mountain road when suddenly the brakes on their car failed.

The car careened almost out of control down the road, bouncing off the crash barriers, until it miraculously ground to a halt scraping along the mountainside. The car's occupants, shaken but unhurt, now had a problem: they were stuck halfway down a mountain in a car with no brakes. What were they to do?

"I know", said the Departmental Manager, "Let's have a meeting, propose a Vision, formulate a Mission Statement, define some Goals, and by a process of Continuous Improvement find a solution to the Critical Problems, and we can be on our way."

"No, no", said the Hardware Engineer, "That will take far too long, and besides, that method has never worked before. I've got my Swiss Army knife with me, and in no time at all I can strip down the car's braking system, isolate the fault, fix it, and we can be on our way."

"Well", said the Software Engineer, "before we do anything, I think we should push the car back up to the top and see if it happens again."

Admittedly, a rather corny joke (you should expect nothing less from me by this point!), but I think it illustrates, at least a little bit, a rather important point: there are different kinds of wisdom, each one stemming from very different sources. And the source of your wisdom will largely determine how effective living by that wisdom will be in any given situation. Choices and decisions that, in one realm, are perfectly appropriate and quite effective, in another area become simply absurd.

And this is the basic concept that James is teaching about in the passage we're focusing on in this chapter. He mentioned the idea of wisdom before, briefly in chapter one of his epistle, and now he comes back to expand on the topic here in chapter three. And in this passage, he highlights two different kinds of wisdom: the wisdom of men and the wisdom of God. For each of these types of wisdom, James gives us three details; he tells us its source, he describes the fruit that it bears in your life and he predicts the ultimate result that will come from following it.

The Wisdom of Man

Let's start by looking at man's wisdom. First of all, where does man's wisdom come from? James tells us that this wisdom is earthly, natural and demonic, of the devil. Most commentators were quick to point out that these refer to the three traditionally recognized external sources of temptation: the world, the flesh and the Devil.

I want to briefly look at each of these ideas a bit more closely. The word James uses for earthly means relating to the physical world, either in a physical or a moral sense, so it is in direct contrast to the spiritual world. This is wisdom that comes from observation and our own understanding, not from revelation. And Scripture is fairly clear about the usefulness of such wisdom: the wisdom of the world is foolishness to God and God's wisdom is foolishness to the world.

However, we must make a distinction here between the wisdom of the world and the knowledge of the world. It is possible for mankind to gain tremendous knowledge about the world; we have, throughout history, increased our understanding to the world and how it works, and we will likely continue to increase in knowledge about the world for as long as God allows us to remain in it. And this is not a bad thing! But it is not the same as wisdom. We discover many things about the world – that is knowledge. It is wisdom that teaches us what to do with that knowledge. And when our source of wisdom is earthly, the way we use our knowledge is often not in line with what God wants for us.

The second source of man's wisdom is a little harder to translate. The NET renders this word as "natural," while the NIV uses "unspiritual" and the King James chooses "sensual." The Greek word literally means, "of or belonging to breath." To the Greeks, this word implied or referred to that part of mankind which we share with the animal kingdom: the instinctive urge we have to satisfy all of our physical desires. Albert Barnes puts it, "It is that which takes counsel of [or is directed by] our natural appetites and propensities."[37]

In other words, this is the wisdom of the "old man," not of the new creation, the wisdom which teaches us to focus on sensual pleasure, on gratifying our physical desires. The wisdom that leads us away from spiritual truth and away from the desires that God has for our lives.

The third source of man's wisdom is a little bit more straightforward: the Devil. Literally, the Greek word used here means, "proceeding from, or resembling, a demon." So, in practical terms, this would be the wisdom that comes from believing the lies that Satan tells. And in some ways, that is really a summary of all the sources of man's wisdom, because Satan is always trying to direct us toward our physical understanding, toward our natural inclinations and desires, trying to direct us away from spiritual or Godly understanding. And I think it is important to note that Satan is extremely good at what he does. He knows very well how to manipulate and deceive people; he's been doing it for a long time. And the wisdom that he directs you to always works against the wisdom of God.

So these are the sources of the wisdom of man as James outlines them for us: the world, which is our intellect or understanding; the flesh, referring to our animalistic, natural desires; and the Devil, the wisdom that leads us to our natural, selfish inclinations and away from God.

Next, James outlines for us the fruit of man's wisdom. Where does man's wisdom lead? James gives us four descriptions. First, it causes us to, **"have bitter jealousy."** These are three interesting words in the Greek. The word for "have" means simply "to have or possess," but in practice, it was the word used to refer to a person's relationship to their spouse: a very close, personal, intimate and important connection, something that you fervently hold on to. The word translated "bitter" has two basic meanings. First, it means something that is acrid, harsh or corrosive. Second, it can refer to something sharp or prickly; I picture a thorn caught in your clothes so that every time you move, it pricks you. Not something deadly or serious, but very annoying. So the idea James is aiming at with this word is a small but incessant discomfort, one that is gradually building, becoming more significant over time because it never lets up.

But the third word, "jealousy," I think is the most interesting of all. Literally, it means, "to boil or glow brightly because of heat." Figuratively, it meant to burn with zeal or with fierce indignation. So the overall picture James is painting here is someone who is desperately, fiercely holding onto a passion that is slowly eating them up like acid.

And that picture ties directly into the description of the second fruit of man's wisdom that James give us: selfishness. The King James translates this word as "strife," while the NIV expands it to "selfish ambition." Originally in the Greek, this was a political term; it meant canvassing for votes, gathering support to try to get yourself elected to some political office. But the connotation was that you were gathering votes in any way you could, legal or otherwise. Aristotle defines this word as "a self-seeking pursuit of political office by unfair means."

The New Testament writers took this political term and began using it metaphorically, meaning "a desire to put one's self forward, or someone with a partisan and fractious spirit." In other words, this is someone who fosters an "us and them" kind of atmosphere, someone who encourages divisions and rivalries so that they can build up their own power and influence.

Notice that these first two phrases James uses to describe the fruit of man's wisdom, when taken together, describe a wisdom that exults man, not God. This is wisdom that encourages us to bitterly despise those who we perceive to be better than we are, wisdom that encourages us to strive for personal power and supremacy, regardless of the cost. Wisdom that teaches us take the best for ourselves, because it teaches us that we are worthy of the best.

And that idea feeds directly into the third fruit that James lists for us: boasting. The word James uses here is the intense form of the basic word meaning "to boast." So this is mega-boasting, or boasting in such a way, or to such an extent, that the reputations or lives of those around you suffer. As some commentators observe, such boasting is only possible in two situations: when we see (or imagine) how much better we are than those around us or when we are seeking to elevate ourselves above those who we think are actually better than we are. In either case, such boasting demonstrates that we are seeking personal glory by comparing our lives to other people. Instead of measuring ourselves against God's standard, as we should, we measure ourselves against those around us.

And the natural result of this kind of boasting is the final fruit that James describes for us: deceit. This is probably the most straightforward word that James uses in these verses; it means simply "to speak falsely" or "to deceive with words." To tell lies. And that, in this context, makes perfect sense. When you are boasting in the way that James has identified in these verses you are essentially seeking to increase their own fame. And when that is your goal, it is often quite impossible to resist coloring the facts to make yourself shine a little brighter. So you begin to tell lies, trying to deceive people into believing you are better than you actually are.

And that is the culmination of this rather bleak description of the results of man's wisdom that James gives us: a person who is consumed by jealousy for the people around them, one who is desperate to be seen as the greatest of them all, a that desperation leads them to boast of how great they are, often stooping to deception and lies in order to make themselves seem greater.

But where does all of this jealousy, ambition and boastful deceit lead? What is the ultimate result of man's wisdom? The answer James gives us in verse 16 is equally bleak: where man's wisdom rules, "**there is disorder and every evil practice.**"

So, here is a basic summary of James' account of man's wisdom. This kind of wisdom is encouraged by Satan and gratifies our natural desires, which leads us to be jealous of other's abilities and achievements and encourages us to exalt ourselves over everyone else, by any means necessary, which causes division and strife, ultimately encouraging every kind of evil practice.

Not a very pretty picture.

The Wisdom of God

Thankfully, James doesn't quit there; he follows up this bleak picture with a description of God's wisdom. First, in verse 17, he tells us where God's wisdom comes from: this is the wisdom that comes from above, from heaven. Other passages of Scripture confirm this idea. In passages like 1 Corinthians 1:24 and 30or Colossians 2:3, Christ is said to be God's wisdom.

Second Timothy 3:15 tells us that God's word makes us wise for salvation. And of course, throughout the book of Proverbs, we learn that the way to gain wisdom is to learn to know God better. So clearly, the wisdom of God comes from above, from knowing God, through His Word and through a living, growing relationship with His Son, Jesus Christ.

And what is the fruit of God's wisdom? James describes several, the first of which is gentleness or humility. I find this rather interesting, because James mentions this idea in verse 13, the first verse of this section: **"Who is wise and understanding among you? By his good conduct he should show his works done in the gentleness that wisdom brings."** So, in essence, James is saying that humility is the defining characteristic, the hallmark of Godly wisdom, which makes perfect sense, when you think about it. Godly wisdom comes from growing closer to God, from knowing Him better, and as we grow closer to God, we see Him more clearly. As we begin to see Him more clearly, how can we help but be appalled by our own wretchedness and wickedness? Anyone who can stand before the throne of God and proudly boast about how great they are obviously isn't seeing God very clearly; that would be like me boasting about my great height (I'm about 5', 6") while standing next to Michael Jordan (who is reportedly about 6', 6"). That just wouldn't work very well! In the same way, someone who is proud or boastful about their own ability or their own greatness is automatically disqualified from Godly wisdom, because the first requirement of Godly wisdom is understanding who you really are in relation to the God of the Universe. And anyone who has truly understood how small and weak they are compared to Him will have a lot of trouble boasting about anything.

So the first, and in some ways the overarching fruit of Godly wisdom is humility, meekness.

Then, in verse 17, James lists eight more results or fruits of Godly wisdom. And it is quite a list: purity, peace, gentleness, submission (being accommodating or thinking of others), mercy, producing good fruit, impartiality, and sincerity (translated in the negative sense in the NET as "not hypocritical").

Now, I have to admit that my first inclination as I was originally preparing this message was to go through and describe each of these words, looking at the Greek that James uses for each one to see what deep truths might have been obscured in the English translation. But I realized pretty quickly as I started to study them that there really isn't any need to do that.

Because, taken together, these words simply describe someone who is living a Christ-like life. This is someone who is growing closer to God, who is listening to God's direction in their life and thus is living as God calls us to live, in submission to Him and, as much as it depends on them, in peace with others. Which is exactly what James suggests will be the ultimate result of God's wisdom. Verse 13 says, in essence, let him who is wise demonstrate it through their Godly life. Following Godly wisdom leads, inevitably, to a life of blessing. Not a life of luxury or a life without trouble and suffering, but rather, as the phrase that James used literally means, "a manner of life made beautiful by reason of purity of heart," or "a life that is genuine, precious and approved by God."

When we live such genuine lives, we become peacemakers, sowing peace in others and reaping a harvest of righteousness.

The Obvious Choice

So, in this passage, James is giving us two pictures of wisdom, and it feels just a little bit redundant to mention that he is suggesting one of these kinds of wisdom might be better than the other. Hopefully that much was clear to you just by reading the verses at the start of this chapter!

But as I close our investigation into this section of James, I do want to point out two things. First, I want to remind you that man's wisdom is what comes naturally to us. To live a life guided by man's wisdom requires that we simply follow our natural inclinations; that kind of wisdom is the default setting of our sinful nature. And, given that the Devil is actively encouraging us in that direction, that is the kind of life we will naturally fall into unless we are intentional about seeking the wisdom of God. And remember the ultimate conclusion of man's wisdom: discord, strife and every kind of evil. That is where our natural wisdom will lead us. And the longer we follow that kind of wisdom, the more of that fruit we will reap in our lives.

But the good news is that God's wisdom is easy to find. Many Eastern religions talk about the path to enlightenment, the path to wisdom, and it involves years of meditation, study and self-deprivation; only the most dedicated, the chosen few, ever find it. But God's wisdom is easy. We simply have to turn away from ourselves and turn to Him. We just have to acknowledge our weakness, our sinfulness, our helplessness, and ask Him to be our strength, to guide us where He would have us go. In other words, we simply have to humble ourselves before Him and ask Him to be Lord of our lives.

Like I said, God's wisdom is easy to find. Not so easy is to follow it consistently in our lives, though, because our sinful nature, our natural inclinations are constantly pulling us in the other direction.

This passage from James is a good reminder of where each of these types of wisdom ultimately leads us, and I hope you are encouraged to persevere in following the wisdom of God. Because when we sow God's wisdom in our lives, we reap the fruit of a blessed life, a life characterized by peace, holiness and joy.

Chapter Fourteen: Conflict, Strife and Humility

James 4: 1 – 10

> **Where do the conflicts and where do the quarrels among you come from? Is it not from this, from your passions that battle inside you? You desire and you do not have; you murder and envy and you cannot obtain; you quarrel and fight. You do not have because you do not ask; you ask and do not receive because you ask wrongly, so you can spend it on your passions.**
>
> **Adulterers, do you not know that friendship with the world means hostility toward God? So whoever decides to be the world's friend makes himself God's enemy. Or do you think the scripture means nothing when it says, "The spirit that God caused to live within us has an envious yearning"? But he gives greater grace. Therefore it says, "God opposes the proud, but he gives grace to the humble." So submit to God. But resist the devil and he will flee from you. Draw near to God and he will draw near to you. Cleanse your hands, you sinners, and make your hearts pure, you double-minded. Grieve, mourn, and weep. Turn your laughter into mourning and your joy into despair. Humble yourselves before the Lord and he will exalt you.**

Years ago when I was thinking about starting a sermon series on the book of James, there were several passages that I was looking forward to diving into. I was eager to have the chance to dig into the passage about favoritism in chapter 2, and some of the verses of encouragement and profound teaching in chapter 1 seemed like they would be wonderful to investigate. But, at the same time, I was very much not looking forward to speaking on these final two chapters; there are some extremely challenging passages in chapters four and five of this epistle!

Perhaps one of the most challenging of these, I think, is the passage we will be focusing on in this chapter – the first ten verses of chapter four. And I feel like I should admit right from the start that there are many things that James says in this passage that I don't understand. If you were expecting or hoping for a full, concise explication of this passage, you should abandon hope right now!

But there are a few ideas that suggest themselves to me from this passage, and I'd like to spend a while looking at them together.

Conflicts and Quarrels

James begins chapter four of his epistle by focusing on conflicts: **"Where do the conflicts and where do the quarrels among you come from?"** The King James renders this phrase as **"wars and fights"** which is actually closer to the meaning of the Greek words that James uses.

There is one idea that jumps out at me about this verse, and that is the context. In the last section of chapter three (the section just before this one), James spent a long time describing Godly wisdom, and his conclusion was that Godly wisdom leads to a life characterized by righteousness, which leads to peace. He makes this connection between peace and righteousness explicit in verse 18, the final verse of chapter three: **And the fruit that consists of righteousness is planted in peace among those who make peace.**

Then, the very next verse, chapter four verse one, asks, "What is causing all the fighting among you?" In the context of what James has expounded in chapter three, wouldn't the obvious answer be the unrighteousness in their lives? The modern practice of dividing Scripture into chapters and verses serves to obscure the connection between these two sentences, but as this letter was read aloud to the original audience, that connection must have been inescapably obvious: those who seek Godly wisdom will live lives of peace, which leads to righteousness. So what's causing these fights and quarrels among you?

Of course, this message is aimed at us just as much as it was at those who first received it. James calls us to seek Godly wisdom, characterized by peace and righteousness. So what do you think might be causing the conflicts in our lives?

However, as is so often the case, James doesn't stop there. He expands on this point by describing two kinds of lives: a life submitted to self-indulgence, which is pleasing to the world, and a life submitted to pleasing God. It is, I think, the contrast between these two kinds of lives that becomes the focus of James' teaching in this passage.

The Life of Self-indulgence
Though he begins by describing the life of self-indulgence, what

James describes in the next verse seems to me to be a small child. He never actually uses that word, but those of you who are parents know what I'm talking about. I can't tell you how many times something like James is describing here has taken place in our house between our children (thankfully less often now that they are all getting a bit older, though when they were smaller, this scene played itself out in our house pretty much daily!). One of them decides they absolutely need some toy, a decision which generally stems from the fact that one of their siblings just picked up said toy. So they demand the toy for themselves, often appealing to the idea of justice: "It is my toy so you have to give it to me!" or "I haven't had a turn with that yet, so you have to give it to me!" But what they really mean, the true impetus behind their desire, is, "I want it!" In a word, selfishness. And of course, the sibling who picked up the toy generally reacts by defending their rights as well. "I get a turn with it too, so I don't have to give it to you!" or "You weren't playing with it, so it is my turn now!" But though they couch their defense in terms of justice as well, what they really mean is, "I don't want to give it up!" In other words, selfishness.

So selfishness meets selfishness in a contest of wills which often quickly escalates into an argument and possibly (depending on how quickly the parent intervenes) erupts into a physical fight.

And that seems to fit perfectly the picture James paints in verse two: **"You desire and you do not have; you murder and envy and you cannot obtain; you quarrel and fight."**

But, once again, James takes this idea one step further by introducing the idea of prayer: **"You do not have because you do not ask; you ask and do not receive because you ask wrongly."** Charles Tyree suggests that James is describing two different kinds of people here. One is the person who trusts completely in their own strength; this is the person who is so confident that God wants what they want that they don't even bother to ask God to fulfill their desires. They just take what they want and try to force their own will on others, which of course, creates tension and divisions and conflicts all around them. And then they wonder why they don't have what they want, why their life is so filled with conflict and strife. James tells them plainly: **"You do not have because you do not ask."**

The other person is one who seeks to manipulate God into getting what they want. They are interested in God only in so far as God can give them what they want, only in so far as He can satisfy their cravings.

Obviously God isn't interested in granting such desires, because, as James says, they want only **"so [they] can spend it on [their] passions."** The King James renders this phrase **"that ye may consume it upon your lusts."** Two of those words caught my attention. The word James uses for "spend" means "to waste," and the word for "passions" means "sensual desire"; it is the word from which we get the English word hedonism. So James is referring here to someone who is begging God to give them what they need to satisfy the wasteful and destructive desires of their sinful nature. And they wonder why God declines!

Then, James changes gears again. As Tyree puts it, "What began as a personal question has now become a personal rebuke." In verse four, James asks, **"Adulterers, do you not know that friendship with the world means hostility toward God?"** I found it interesting that the original Greek word used here is actually quite specific. Literally, James says, "You adulterers and adulteresses." He wanted to make sure they knew he wasn't speaking just to a particular group or class of people; he meant everyone. And his choice of metaphor, adultery, is also quite revealing. Throughout their history, the Jews regularly referred to their covenant with God as a spiritual marriage; the prophets often talk of idolaters in terms of adultery, and the early church picked up the same metaphor to describe being faithful to Christ, choosing to love God above all else. So essentially, James is accusing his readers of choosing their love for the world over their commitment to and relationship with God, making them guilty of adultery.

This metaphor would have resonated strongly with the Jews reading this letter. But even stronger is the dichotomy that James sets up in the rest of verse four: **"friendship with the world means hostility toward God."** One thing that strikes me about this statement is the strength of the words that James uses. The word for friendship, both times it is used in verse four is *philos*, which means either "friendship" or "a fondness for," which makes sense in this context. But the word translated here as "hostility" is a form of the word that is translated as "enemy" in the second half of the verse. The second word, "enemy" is the root word which means either "something that is hateful, odious" or, when used as a noun, "an adversary." If you are thinking that sounds a bit familiar to you, you're right, you have heard this word before. It is the word most often used in Scripture to describe, or in some cases to name, Satan.

I think Albert Barnes has a great summary, both of what James means by "the world" and what friendship with the world refers to. He says,

> The term world here is to be understood as… the
> community, or people, called "the world," in
> contradistinction from the people of God. The "friendship
> of the world," is the love of that world; of the maxims
> which govern it, the principles which reign there, the ends
> that are sought, the amusements and gratifications which
> characterize it as distinguished from the church of God. It
> consists in setting our hearts on those things; in conforming
> to them; in making them the object of our pursuit with the
> same spirit with which they are sought by those who make
> no pretensions to religion.[38]

So James is saying that anyone who fits that description, who is fond of the world in that way, is the enemy of God. That may sound rather harsh to some of us today, until you put it in the terms that James does: adultery. If this was referring to physical, actual adultery, there is no question of the truth of James' statement. I have heard of couples who survive an adulterous affair; it takes tremendous work and an unwavering commitment to the marriage to surmount such a violation, but some people have managed it. But can you imagine a couple surviving an affair if the adulterer refused to give up the affair? If they continued to be unfaithful to their spouse, could the marriage possibly survive? That is the kind of situation James is describing: a believer who is seeking to protect and maintain their intimacy with the world while, at the same time, remaining in fellowship with God. And it just doesn't work! Such an attitude is hateful, odious to God, just as it would be for a human spouse in such a circumstance.

So this is the first picture that James gives us: a believer who is selfishly seeking to gratify their own desires because they have become enamored of the world, thus committing spiritual adultery against God, making them a constant source of conflict and strife within the church. And then comes verse five: **Or do you think the scripture means nothing when it says, "The spirit that God caused to live within us has an envious yearning"?** This is one of those things that I just don't quite understand in this passage. And apparently I'm in good company; the commentators I read had many different interpretations of what James says here, as well as many different explanations for how he manages to quote a verse from Scripture that no one has been able to find in Scripture! The prevailing opinion on that question, by the way, is that James is not actually quoting here at all; he is giving a summary of the Old Testament as a whole. As Barnes puts it, "he meant to refer to what was the current teaching or general spirit of the Old Testament."[39]

But ultimately all of these explanations and commentaries ended with some kind of statement that essentially meant, "We don't know what this means." In fact, many of the commentaries I read just skipped it entirely, ignoring verse five and moving happily on to verse six. And that, unfortunately, is the best that I can do as well; though it bothers me to admit it, this is one of those statements in Scripture that I'm going to have to wait until Heaven to figure out!

The Life Submitted to God

In verse six, James begins to describe the other half of the picture he is painting in this passage, and this is not the kind of picture that I was expecting. In the last three verses of this section, James gives about ten different commands, commands which, if you take them out of context, seem quite odd. He tells us: submit to God; resist the devil, and he will flee from you; draw near to God and he will draw near to you; cleanse your hands, you sinners; make your hearts pure, you double minded; grieve, mourn and weep; turn your laughter into morning and your joy into despair; and finally, humble yourselves before the Lord, and He will exalt you.

At this point, I don't want to take the time to go through each of these commands one at a time, but I do want to point out three observations. First, I think it is worth mentioning that the commands in verse nine, **"Grieve, mourn, and weep. Turn your laughter into mourning and your joy into despair. Humble yourselves before the Lord and he will exalt you,"** these attitudes ought not to be the norm for the Christian life; that's not what James is suggesting here. He's not commanding us as believers to go through life with our eyes on the ground, a perpetual frown on our face and a tear in our eye, continually mourning our sins and just generally being depressed all the time. No, Christ calls us to live a life of abundance and joy in Him. These attitudes that James commands are appropriate, however, when we are confronted with the sinfulness of our lives. While we should seek joy in our lives (considering all we have gained in Christ!), we should also, even in the midst of our joy, be horrified and chagrined when considering the continued sinfulness of our hearts and desires. In that context, these attitudes of mourning, despair and humility are not only appropriate – they're essential if we hope to find freedom from the chains of sin which still cling to us.

Which leads into my second observation: the list of commands that James gives in this passage presupposes guilt. The people James was writing to must have been struggling with this issue; he seems to assume that they are committing spiritual adultery, that they are submitting themselves to the fulfillment of their own selfish desires. So these commands that James lists are the path to repentance; if you struggle with spiritual adultery, this is the cure! And the key is submission and humility, recognizing that you have nothing to be proud of, that your accomplishments and your abilities are liabilities and idols, then humbly purifying your heart and your life, drawing near to God in submission to His will.

Which brings us to my third observation: the whole point of these commands is the restoration of our relationship with God. He doesn't care how dirty we are or how we have violated our covenant with Him. If we will repent of our sin and humble ourselves before Him, He will draw near to us and He will lift us up.

Hope for All Adulterers

What an amazing picture that is! A picture of a God who sees all that we are, who sees our adulterous hearts, sees our selfishness and the unrighteousness in our lives that stirs up contention and strife all around us and yet who still freely offers forgiveness and restoration to all who will come to Him.

I think one reason James was so confident that his readers were struggling with this issue is that we all struggle with it, to one degree or another. All of us have given a part of our heart away to the things of this world; all of us have, in small or big ways, put our own selfish desires on the throne of our lives; all of us deserve the condemnation found in verse four. We are adulterous people, each one of us, in our own personal ways.

But praise be to God, there is a cure for our wandering hearts! Submit yourself to God. Repent and purify your heart. Draw near to Him and He will draw near to you. Humble yourself before Him and He will lift you up.

What a joy it would be if He would make this kind of repentance true in all of hearts, in every area of our lives today, that peace and righteousness might reign in our lives as we faithfully serve our King!

Chapter Fifteen: Do Not Judge

James 4: 11 – 12

> **Do not speak against one another, brothers and sisters. He who speaks against a fellow believer or judges a fellow believer speaks against the law and judges the law. But if you judge the law, you are not a doer of the law but its judge. But there is only one who is lawgiver and judge – the one who is able to save and destroy. On the other hand, who are you to judge your neighbor?**

When I originally wrote this message, I wanted very much to find a joke to open it with. Now, I have failed to find that joke twice; I didn't find it back then and I didn't find one now either. Which is a shame, because I think a little humor here would help a lot; we are moving into another of those very difficult sections in the book of James. In fact, John MacArthur says that these verses strike "at the very heart of… how we perceive sin."[40] And that perception shapes our view of righteousness, shapes how we relate to God and how we relate to those around us. Kind of a heavy topic. Too bad I couldn't find a joke to open up with.

Take a moment to read over the verses printed above one more time. Step through this passage slowly and carefully. There is some very deep theology in these verses, and obviously I can't begin to cover everything that James is teaching here, if for no other reason than I'm sure I don't *know* everything that James is teaching here! But I do want to mention a few points that jump out at me.

The Basics: Do not Slander

First, let's look at the basic meaning of the passage. James gives us a fairly straightforward command in this passage: Do not speak against your brothers and sisters in Christ. Now, as usual, the first thing that strikes me is the words James uses, and the key word in the first part of verse 11 is the verb rendered in the NET as "speak against," which the NIV translates "slander." The Greek word is *katalaleo*, which is one of those interesting Greek words that defies easy definition. The basic meaning is "to speak against," but it is a compound word, formed from two different Greek words. The first, *kata*, simply means "against." But the second, *laleho*, is one of the two Greek words that meant speaking. The other is *lego*, which is a form of the word *logos*, and it refers to speech that is logical or meaningful. *Laleho*, on the other hand, simply refers to sounds coming out of the mouth. It was often used to describe the sounds that animals make; when applied to human speech, it denoted mindless, thoughtless speech. A good English synonym would be "babble."

So James is referring to careless or thoughtless babble that runs other people down, that denigrates others. In other words, slander. The technical definition of slander is, "the utterance in the presence of another person of a false statement or statements, damaging to a third person's character or reputation."[41] Just briefly I want you to note the three components that make up slander. It is a statement or statements made publically, to another person. These statements are false, and they are damaging to another person's character.

All of that, in the first part of verse 11, is what James is forbidding: do not slander each other. Seems fairly straightforward, doesn't it? I mean, that's a pretty obvious thing that we ought not to do, especially to others within the church. It kind of ranks right up there with not running with scissors, right?

And I think, because it is so obvious, there is a tendency for us to minimize the significance of this sin. Of course we shouldn't gossip and speak badly of each other. But did you see what Bob did yesterday? Did you hear what Nancy said? And we think, if we think of it at all, that because we're just talking, because it is just words, it's not that big a deal.

There is a great illustration in the Old Testament of how serious this sin can be. The story begins in 2 Samuel 10. The king of the Ammonites has died, and his son Hanun replaces him on the throne. The old king had been kind to King David, so David decides to send a delegation to Hanun, expressing his condolences. The delegation arrives and Hanun's advisers say, "Do you really think David sent these guys to show his sympathy? They're here to scout out the city, so David can come and conquer it!" In other words, these advisors slander David, casting doubt on his character and his motives. Hanun trusts his advisers, so he takes David's delegation and shaves off half their beards, cuts their robes in half so they're half naked and then sends them home. Now, though it is fairly obvious this wasn't a complementary thing for Hunan to do, the full import of this action is lost to us, being so far removed from ancient Jewish culture. This was extremely disgraceful; to be seen in such a condition would have been utterly humiliating for these people, the kind of humiliation that you don't ever recover from. And of course, because David sent them as his official delegation, essentially Hanun was doing this disgraceful thing to David himself. When these men get back to Israel and David treats them as kindly as he can; he sends word that they are to stay in Jericho (right on the border of Israel) in hiding and seclusion until their beards grow back. But, even with David's best efforts, it is rather a case of too little, too late. The damage has already been done.

Scripture doesn't tell us specifically how David reacted emotionally to this extreme insult leveled at him by Hanun, but we can make a fairly educated guess, because in the very next verse after we hear about how David treated the returning delegation, we see the Ammonites hiring an army of Arameans to fight for them; apparently, they realized their actions had made them a serious enemy! When David hears they've hired an army, he sends out his army to fight them. In the ensuing battle, the Aramean mercenaries flee from the army of Israel, which causes the Ammonites to flee also. David chases down the Arameans and slaughters them, killing their king. Then, he sends his army against the Ammonites and slaughters them as well.

The important thing to note in this story, at least as it pertains to this passage in James, is that no one involved wanted a war. David was looking to show sympathy to the Ammonites. The Ammonites weren't ready to fight Israel, or they wouldn't have hired mercenaries to fight for them. And the Arameans certainly had nothing against Israel. But because of one slanderous word, about fifty thousand people died in two wars that devastated two kingdoms!

Speaking carelessly about others can have very serious consequences.

And in case we haven't gotten the message yet, James continues in the second half of verse 11: **"He who speaks against a fellow believer or judges a fellow believer speaks against the law and judges the law."** Now, in case you were wondering, James uses the same word twice in the last half of verse 11, and both times it is the same word we talked about in the first half of this verse: *katalaleo* – thoughtless, denigrating babble. But more than that, I want you to notice here how James ups the ante a little bit. In the second half of this verse, he adds the idea of judging each other. Not only should we not speak against or slander each other, we should not judge each other either.

Again, I think the words are significant. The word James uses for "judge" here is *krino*, which means "to condemn." We're not talking about evaluation or constructive criticism; we're talking about condemnation. And I think this progression is a critical part of what James is trying to communicate here. When you speak against others, when you gossip and slander those around you, you are moving yourself into the seat of judgment. You are necessarily appointing yourself as their judge and jury; often, you become their executioner as well, at least as far as their reputation goes. This progression is the natural, inevitable consequence of speaking against others: you wind up standing in judgment against them.

A Brief Clarification

Now, at this point, I think it is important to pause for a moment to clarify exactly what James is saying and what he is *not* saying in this verse. This clarification is necessary because many people have suggested that in this verse, James is contradicting other passages in Scripture, places where we are commanded to judge the motives and actions of others, even those within the church, as well as those places where we are pretty clearly commanded to publically speak out against others.

Let me make two observations about those other passages. First, in every case, those passages are dealing with sin in the church. When believers are living in sin, when they are obdurately holding onto their sinful lifestyle, even after being confronted by the church, then we are commanded to speak out against them, in the hope of restoring them to righteousness and fellowship within the church. And that brings up the second observation: the goal of this kind of speaking out is always restoring fellowship, speaking the truth in love, in the hope that our brother or sister might turn from their sin, repent and be restored to fellowship with God and with the church.

That kind of speaking out, that kind of discerning judgment, is frequently affirmed in Scripture. And that kind of speaking out is emphatically not what James is talking about in these verses. In fact, you could make a case that James is actually practicing that kind of speaking out in these in these very verses. He is in the process of pointing out habitual sin in the lives of his readers in the hope of calling them back into the righteous life that God requires of them.

Conversely, the speaking out that he is condemning here has nothing to do with love or reconciliation. The speaking out that James is referring to here differs from the speaking out that is commanded in two important aspects: the circumstances and the motivation. The implication of slander, as James describes it, is that the speaking is public but the victim is absent. You are not going to someone privately, seeking to help them by rebuking sin in their life. No, you are going to others, publically defaming this other person's character or their actions. Now, there may be sin involved, or there may not be. But the crux of the issue is that you do not take the problem to its source, seeking reconciliation. You take the report to others, which can only result in discord and strife and condemnation. And this brings out the difference in motivations. The goal of speaking out which Scripture affirms is always reconciliation, drawing believers out of sin and back into fellowship. The motivation is love. The goal of the slander that James is describing (and condemning) is to denigrate, to tear others down, to break fellowship. That means the motivation for this kind of speaking out can only be one of two things: hatred or pride. Either you are seeking revenge for something, real or imagined, that the person has done to you, or you feel you are so much better (or you want to give the impression that you are) than the person you are speaking out against that you feel justified in your right to stand in judgment over them.

That is really what this sin boils down to: hatred and pride. Treating those around us with hatred and contempt rather than with love and forgiveness; acting in pride and arrogance rather than in humility. When you look at it that way, suddenly this little sin of gossip, of speaking against others, doesn't seem quite so harmless, does it? Remember, Jesus taught that what comes out of our mouths reflects what resides in our hearts. When we speak hateful, proud words that tear down those around us, what does that say about what is residing in our heart?

Here Comes the Judge

Then we come to verse 12: "**But there is only one who is lawgiver and judge – the one who is able to save and destroy. On the other hand, who are you to judge your neighbor?**" As we've seen him do many times in this letter already, once again James uses this verse to set up a comparison, in this case, a comparison between two kinds of judges. On the one hand, we have us: those who speak against others in the way that James has described it in verse 11, those who set themselves up as the judges of those around them. Then, on the other hand, James gives us the true Judge: the one who is able to save and destroy, which is, obviously, only God Himself. Any time you find yourself being compared to God, you know you're not going to come out looking very favorable!

But what I find most interesting about this comparison is what James doesn't say. The basis for the comparison is power, the ability to enforce judgments. Over here, we have the Lawgiving and the Judge, the omniscient, omnipotent, omnipresent Creator God of the universe. The One who is able to discern who should be saved and who should be condemned, and the One who has the power to carry out His judgments. And over here, there's us. James doesn't even bother to list all of our inadequacies as judges compared to God. He doesn't point out our limited wisdom, our incomplete knowledge, our faulty assumptions, our impure motives. He only asks a question. But it is a question that really says it all: who are you to judge your neighbor?

That's a question that is worth answering. I think that everyone struggles with this sin, to one degree or another. There are times when each of us is willing to speak (or is at least tempted to speak) against someone else, setting ourselves up as their judge and thus violating the royal law of love that Christ gave: love your neighbor as yourself.

I want to encourage you to take a moment, right now, to consider your conversation. Consider how much of what you say each day falls into the category of speaking against those around you. If you don't like the answer to that question, I would encourage you to spend some time right now, before you move on to whatever is next in your day, confessing and repenting to God. Submit this area of your life to Him and allow His Holy Spirit to begin to transform your speech, that you might begin to relate to others around you as Christ desires His children to: showing grace and love, in humility considering others as more important than ourselves.

Chapter Sixteen: Who Do You Trust?

James 4: 13 – 17

> Come now, you who say, "Today or tomorrow we will go
> into this or that town and spend a year there and do
> business and make a profit." You do not know about
> tomorrow. What is your life like? For you are a puff of
> smoke that appears for a short time and then vanishes.
> You ought to say instead, "If the Lord is willing, then we
> will live and do this or that." But as it is, you boast in your
> arrogance. All such boasting is evil. So whoever knows
> what is good to do and does not do it is guilty of sin.

Charles Tyree tells a story about a man who planted a garden. He took a plot that had been neglected for a long time; it was overgrown and full of weeds. He cleared it, then planted vegetables in neat, straight rows. He watered them, weeded them and took meticulous care of them. As a result, the plants yielded a great harvest. After this great harvest, the man's wife, who was a devout Christian, stood up in the midst of a praise service in church and began to thank God and praise Him for the wonderful garden that He had provided for them. After her rather lengthy words of praise to God, her husband, who looked rather unhappy, stood up. With a sour look on his face, his only comment was, "You should have seen the garden when God had it all to Himself!"

A rather simplistic story, perhaps, but it illustrates well the two attitudes that James is highlighting for us in the passage we are looking at in this chapter. This is another of those passages where James gives us two contrasting pictures, in this case, pictures of two different people. One is of a person who feels they are in charge of their life, the other of a person who has surrendered their life, their plans, their future, to the Lord's guidance. And through these two pictures, James is illustrating three basic principles, principles which I would like to focus our attention on in this chapter.

The First Principle

The first principle James highlights for us is the uncertainty of life, which is the essence of the first picture James paints in verses 13 – 14. Now, the commentaries I read were very quick to point out that James is not simply harping on businessmen here. The example he gives is of merchants preparing their next business trip, an image that would have been very familiar for his audience. This was the typical way for Jewish merchants to do business. They would gather their goods together and take them to a city where they hoped those goods were in demand. Then, they would remain in that city until they had sold everything they brought, after which they would buy new goods and move on to another city. And they would follow this process, sometimes for years, moving from city to city until at last they returned home. And if they had planned well, they would return with much greater wealth then when they departed.

So the specific picture that James paints would have resonated with his original audience; they were likely quite used to hearing merchants speak in the way James describes in these verses. In fact, undoubtedly some of the believers hearing this letter actually were merchants of just this type. But it would be foolish to assume that James is speaking only to people who buy and sell things; it seems fairly clear, from the details in the rest of the passage, that James is using merchants as a specific example. The general idea he wants to communicate is applicable to anyone who makes plans for the future.

And that picture is of someone who, as Albert Barnes puts it, "speaks confidently of what [they] will do in the future."[42] And, as always, I'm immediately drawn to the words James uses. He starts out with an interesting phrase. The NET (as well as the RSV) renders it, "Come now." In the NIV, it is "Now listen," while the King James translates it as "Go to now." Barnes describes it as, "a phrase designed to arrest attention, as if there were something that demanded their notice."[43] So James starts out this section with the linguistic equivalent of waving his arms and shouting, "This is important! Pay attention! You need to hear this!"

And look at the words that follow, a dialogue James puts into the mouth of a hypothetical, but all too familiar, merchant: **"Today or tomorrow we will go into this or that town and spend a year there and do business and make a profit."** Now, I don't know if people really said things like this, if this is realistic dialogue or if James is simply exaggerating a bit to make his point. But notice the focus in this verse. We will go… We will spend a year there… We will do business… We will make a profit. The attitude behind these words is one of utter self-reliance. I have made these plans, and I have the strength to carry them out.

Then, in verse 14, James lets reality burst in on this rosy picture our merchant has painted for himself, and the result, of course, is devastating. **"You do not know about tomorrow. What is your life like? For you are a puff of smoke that appears for a short time and then vanishes."**

There are two important truths that James sets in opposition to the self sufficient attitude. First, the painfully obvious fact that we don't know the future. It is all well and good to say, "Tomorrow we're going to do…" whatever. But we don't even know what will happen in the next hour; we might not live to see the end of this day. Just today at lunch, I had an interesting conversation with my children. My daughter noticed a bottle of wine in the small wine rack we have and she asked me when we were going to drink it. That bottle is one of two bottles that my wife, Lori, and I purchased back in the year we were married (1991, for those of you who are curious); we drank the first on our 20th anniversary and we've been saving the other to drink together on one of our future anniversaries. So, the conversation turned to the question, "Which anniversary will you drink it on? Will you wait until your 50th?" My answer was, "Well, since there's a reasonable chance that one of us won't make it to our 50th anniversary, we might choose to drink it sooner, so that one of us won't have to drink it alone." The kids were not happy with that admission of my mortality, nor of the uncertainty of how long I will continue to be alive. But that is the reality of our situation here on earth: we don't know what will happen tomorrow, and we don't have any guarantee that we will *have* a tomorrow! So confidently asserting that we *will* do a certain thing tomorrow or the next day is patently absurd.

The truth of this was firmly impressed on me several years ago. I was driving home after an evening event at RFIS with my two sons, Josiah and Daniel. I remember thinking that when I got home, I would spend some time relaxing with Lori, maybe watching a video or something. Then I'd go to sleep and get some rest, because I had a drama rehearsal scheduled for early the next morning. There was no place in my confident plans for the three armed robbers to enter our compound, threaten our lives, shoot my friend in the leg and steal from us. But that is what the future held for me that particular night. And my confident plans, "This is what I'll do when I get home," were utterly powerless to change what actually happened.

That is the situation we are always in; we are always utterly powerless to predict the future, because the future is utterly unpredictable.

And that is closely related to the second truth that I find in this first principle: our lives are fragile and uncertain. James uses three powerful words to express this concept in the second half of verse 14. The first is *atmis*, which means "mist or vapor;" this word forms the first part of the English word "atmosphere." The second is *phaino*, meaning "to flicker or briefly appear;" it can also refer to an illusion, something that seems to be there but really isn't. And finally is *aphanizo*, which means either "to be consumed" or "to vanish utterly." The combination of these three words is James' assessment of our lives. We are like a mist that briefly appears and then is consumed, vanishing utterly. The image he may be pointing to is of a candle that has just been blown out; a thin trail of smoke appears for a few moments and then dissipates, though he could just as easily have been thinking of one of the many places in Scripture where our lives are compared to mist or smoke that vanishes away, emphasizing our extremely transitory nature.

But in any case, the point here is fairly obvious: our lives are as fragile and brief as the morning mist, so how can we confidently build plans, when all our plans depend on the continuance of our lives? That is like building our plans on candle smoke; everything will be fine, as long as that smoke doesn't stop! But it will stop, and quickly too. Our lives are just like that, and if we have only ourselves to rely on, this would be a very depressing passage, because James make it abundantly clear that, in the face of life's uncertainties, we are utterly helpless.

The Second Principle

But thankfully, he doesn't stop there; he continues to outline a second principle: to us, life is uncertain, but God is in control of life. This is the second picture that James paints for us in these verses. First, we see the false confidence and plans of self-reliance. Then, in contrast, James says, **"You ought to say instead, "If the Lord is willing, then we will live and do this or that."**

Now, I have to admit that I've never really liked James' answer here. The problem is that we make our plans as if we have the power to make them happen, when in reality we are utterly powerless in an utterly unpredictable world. And, taken at face value, the solution seems to be for us to simply tack the phrase, "If it is the Lord's will" on the front of what we plan to do, making everything fine.

Really, I have two objections to the phrase James suggests. For some, this phrase "Lord willing" has become like a mantra, a meaningless phrase that is used as a kind of good luck charm or magic word that we hope will ensure the success of what we want to do. We know we ought not to make our own plans, so we throw that phrase in to make us feel like we're acknowledging and following God's will before charging ahead with making our own plans. Though I don't know enough about Islam to say this confidently, I have heard others suggest that the typical Muslim phrase "*Insha'Allah*"(which is Arabic for "If God wills it") functions in this way, as a kind of divine rubber stamp on their plans.

For other people, this phrase is used as a shield for their lack of faith. I will always remember sitting in a college youth group meeting many years ago. We were praying for someone who was seriously ill. The father (if I remember correctly) of one member of the group was dying of cancer, and the doctors had just recently declared that he was beyond medicine's ability to help him. So we were praying for him, and I remember getting frustrated because everyone seemed to be praying for him to be comfortable and in peace while he waited to die. Of course, there was nothing wrong with those sentiments, but I wanted him to get better! So when I prayed, I asked God to just heal him; I don't remember my exact words, but the basic intent was, "God, you are able to heal him and we ask you to do just that." And as soon as I finished, someone sitting next to me quickly amended, "Yes Lord, heal him *if it is Your will*." In the context of the meeting, it was painfully obvious that he was correcting my prayerful faux pas. The trouble was that most people in the room didn't believe God would heal him; medical science had failed, so obviously he was going to die. But theologically, they had to acknowledge that God, being omnipotent, *could* heal him. And the tension was, since I had prayed for his healing, what were they to do when he died? Would that mean that God had failed or was somehow unable to heal him? So they used that phrase, "Lord willing," to cover their faithless prayers. When he died, they could comfortably say, "Well, it wasn't in God's will for him to be healed." In other words, "if it is Your will" really meant, "we know You're not going to do this."

So when James holds this up as the alternative to the self-reliant attitude described in this passage, I am a bit disappointed. But of course,

James is thinking of more than simply words. He isn't suggesting that we simply amend our speech with periodic recitations of the phrase, "Lord willing." Rather, he is aiming at a change in attitude. Remember what both Christ and James have taught about our speech? What comes out of our mouths is a reflection of what resides in our hearts. That means that the self-reliant merchant of verses 13 – 14 only cares about their own will for the future; they don't particularly care what God might will for their life. The speech of the person James holds up in verse 15 reflects a heart that is seeking God's will first. My plans will succeed if they match what God has planned for me, and if they don't, then I'm going to change them to suit His plan.

The essential difference here is the attitude, the willingness to acknowledge our absolute dependence on God for absolutely everything. As Solomon puts it in Psalm 127, **"If the Lord does not build a house, then those who build it work in vain."** Or, as Barnes says,

> We need not travel far in life to see how completely all
> that we have is in the hands of God, or to learn how
> easily he can frustrate us if he pleases. There is nothing
> on which the success of our plans depends over which
> we have absolute control; there is nothing, therefore, on
> which we can base the assurance of success but his
> favour.[44]

So James is not suggesting that we must simply repeat this phrase as a magic word to make God bless our plans. Rather, we should always recognize our dependence on Him and lay our plans accordingly.

The Third Principle

And that leads nicely into the final principle that James gives us in this passage: we must surrender our lives to God's sovereignty. James expresses this idea in the negative in verse 16: **"But as it is, you boast in your arrogance. All such boasting is evil."** The idea, as I see it, is this. When we speak as if we are able to accomplish all we've planned; when we imply that our strength is sufficient for all we need; when we speak as if we are in charge of the universe; in those moments, we are boasting, taking God's rightful place for our own. In essence, we are claiming that we don't need God, and that we can do better on our own; remember the garden when God had it to Himself?

James has a very clear, very concise assessment of this kind of boasting: sin. God will not share His glory with anyone, and anyone who tries to take that glory, by word or by deed, intentionally or inadvertently, is sharing in the same evil attitude that changed the great angel Lucifer into the great accuser Satan.

That may seem a little harsh to you. I mean, we're just talking about planning ahead; everyone has to make plans for the future! In fact, there are places in Scripture that command us to plan ahead. Of course we all know that God is in control of things; we understand that our plans can only succeed if they are in line with His will. So really, what is the big deal?

That reaction, I think, illustrates the problem with this issue. Because it is so easy for us to minimize this problem, because it doesn't seem like a big deal; so, I forgot to add "Lord willing" when I talked about my plans, so sue me! The attitude, the feeling that this isn't a very big deal, makes it very easy for self-reliance to creep into our hearts. Because, at bottom, we really *want* to be self-reliant, and I think at least part of the reason why we are so quick to make light of this issue is that, if we genuinely take it seriously, we will be required to give up, forever, all hope of ever being self-reliant.

A Proverb to Remember

And that is why I think James ends this section of his epistle with the proverb of verse 17: "**So whoever knows what is good to do and does not do it is guilty of sin.**" Obviously, this verse has applications far beyond the truth of this particular passage. But I think James uses it as a powerful reminder about this issue. You know that in your speech, you must acknowledge God's sovereignty, and when you don't, you sin.

Though this is a critical truth for all believers, for those of us who work in full time Christian ministry, I think this reminder is especially important. It is very easy for us to begin to imagine that , because we are working for His Kingdom, God must bless our plans. We may never express it in so many words, but often, there is that sense, lingering just at the edge of our awareness, that He *ought* to make this plan work, because we're doing it for Him! Not to mention that nagging frustration, sometimes articulated but always felt, when He blocks our plans; our hearts cry out, "But we were doing this for You!"

It is only a very small, very easy step from that attitude to the belief that God somehow needs us to accomplish His plans. Did you see that garden when God had it all to Himself? He was lucky I came along to fix it up for Him! Translated into real world ministry terms, that statement might easily become, "If not for our years of sacrifice and service, that particular translation of Scripture would never have been completed," or "Just think of all the people who have come to know the Lord because of my ministry."

Now, we may never actually say those words, but I think there is always a temptation to lean in that direction, even if just in our attitudes. Satan is always right next to us in our times of success, encouraging us to take the glory for ourselves, encouraging us to believe that God needs us, that whatever we have accomplished could never have been done without our personal efforts. And I think there are times when we believe those whispered lies, when we allow this attitude of self-reliance to creep into our hearts. And in those times, at least in our minds, we take God off the throne and place ourselves there.

And that is really the heart of this issue: claiming for ourselves the place of God in our lives. Saying, "My will be done, whether God wills it or not." When those moments come, I would encourage you to turn back to this passage and cling to the bitter but important truths that James gives us here.

You are a puff of smoke that appears for a short time and then vanishes.

Whoever knows what is good to do and does not do it is guilty of sin.

Acknowledge God's sovereignty in your life and in your plans; submit your future to His will, as He reveals it to you, so that the words of your mouth and the attitude of your heart might be pleasing to Him.

James 5: 1 – 6

Come now, you rich! Weep and cry aloud over the miseries that are coming on you. Your riches have rotted and your clothing has become moth-eaten. Your gold and silver have rusted and their rust will be a witness against you. It will consume your flesh like fire. It is in the last days that you have hoarded treasure! Look, the pay you have held back from the workers who mowed your fields cries out against you, and the cries of the reapers have reached the ears of the Lord of hosts. You have lived indulgently and luxuriously on the earth. You have fattened your hearts in a day of slaughter. You have condemned and murdered the righteous person, although he does not resist you.

We come in this chapter, to another of those troubling passages in James, the first six verses of chapter 5. I find this passage interesting, not because of what James says, but because of what he doesn't say. First of all, there is no indication here that he is addressing believers. When he spoke of rich people back in chapter one, they were called "brothers," a word which almost all New Testament scholars agree is a form of address that was exclusively reserved for followers of Christ. But in this passage, there is no such indication. Though the word for "rich people" is the same as the one used in chapter 1, here in chapter 5 it is used alone. Not "our rich bothers" but just "rich people." So, the general consensus among the commentators that I read was that, for the first time in this letter, James seems to be turning away from his audience, Jewish Christians, and for these few verses, begins to address rich people in general, those who were wealthy outside of the church.

The second oddity in this passage is that there is no mirror image. Over and over again in this epistle, we've seen James present us with two contrasting images. Usually one is very negative, standing as a warning or admonition, while the other is something positive that God desires for our lives, in essence the "right answer" to whatever problem or circumstance that James is currently addressing. But here in the first section of chapter 5, there is no mirror image. James calls out the rich for their wicked behavior, condemning them in a manner that is strikingly similar to the prophets of the Old Testament. And then he moves on; no brighter image to lead them back to righteousness, no hint that there is any hope of redemption for them. Just the certainty of future judgment because of their sinful actions.

I don't know about you, but I find that rather troubling. So I started digging into this passage, hoping to figure out exactly what James is trying to teach us here in these verses.

Who are The Rich?

The first detail I examined was who, exactly, James is addressing in this passage. Now, on one level, that's kind of an obvious question, right? He's talking to "the rich;" he comes right out and says that in the first phrase of verse one. But clearly, this being James, there is more to it than just that. He identifies the rich people he has in mind by listing four behaviors that they participate in. First, they hoard their wealth, storing it up instead of using it for the good others. Second, they keep their wealth from others by refusing to pay their workers the wages they promised to pay. Third, they spend their wealth on luxurious living. And finally, they use the power that their wealth gives them to oppress others.

Not a very pretty picture. But there are two details about this picture that I find even more troubling than the description. First is the lack of the word "brothers" when addressing these rich people. As I mentioned before, all of the commentators that I read took this as an absolute sign that James was speaking to unbelieving Jews, or even to Gentiles; he didn't call these rich people "brothers" so they must not be Christians. And that would fine, except for the fact that the commentators are wrong. You see, the trouble is that you can't prove a negative, only a positive. Let me try to explain with an absurd example. Suppose you wanted to prove that I can not fly. How would you do it? You could list all of the times you have not seen me fly (assuming you have ever seen me do anything; remember, it's a hypothetical example!) You could talk about the times you've known me to travel by conventional means, theorizing that, if I could fly, I wouldn't spend my time fighting through Yaoundé traffic in a car (traffic in this capital city of Cameroon is legendary, not to be braved by the faint of heart!) or that I wouldn't bother taking an airplane when I need to travel between the States and Cameroon. If you were very determined, you could come find me, take me up to the roof of a tall building and throw me off, then watch to see what I do. But even so, you still wouldn't have proven that I can't fly; you would only have proven that you've never seen me fly. Even the rooftop trick wouldn't do it, because it might be that not revealing my secret ability is more important than saving my life, so even in that circumstance, my not flying does not prove that I can't fly; it only proves that I didn't fly.

On the other hand, if we happened to meet up in a restaurant somewhere and, just before the check arrives, I step away from our table, lift off and soar out the window into the sky, then you could say conclusively that you've proven that I can fly (you could also be annoyed that I stuck you with paying the check, but that's not important right now). In other words, you would have proven a positive: that I can fly. But you really can't ever prove the negative.

So how does all of this apply to this verse in James? The commentators assume that because James did not use the word "brothers" in chapter 5, he is not addressing rich believers as he did in chapter 1. But that assumption is an attempt to prove a negative, that James is *not* addressing rich believers. Given the evidence we have, you can't prove that statement. If he had used the word "brothers" as he does in chapter 1, then we could definitively say that he is addressing only rich believers or if he had said, "All rich people who are not followers of Christ," we could confidently say he is not addressing rich believers. But as it is, all we can really say is that James does not specify any particular kind of rich person. He isn't only talking to rich believers, but that doesn't mean that he isn't talking to them at all.

So why is this minor point, which I'm making into a major discussion, so troubling? Simply this: since we can't be sure James is speaking only to unbelieving rich people, there is at least a chance that this passage applies equally to rich people within the church.

The second troubling aspect of this picture is the word James uses for "rich people." In Greek, this is the word *plousios*, which generally means, "abounding in material resources." But it was also commonly used in a metaphorical sense, in which case it meant, "abundantly supplied" or "having everything that you need."

Think for a moment about what these two facts mean. The rich people James is addressing are not necessarily just people outside of the church; James could very well be speaking to wealthy people within the church. And the definition of "rich person" is "anyone who has all that they need." This

brings me to an inescapable conclusion: I'm rich! And chances are most of
you are too. That makes me a little bit more interested in what James has to
say to these rich people in this passage.

The Sins of The Rich

The trouble is, James' message for these "rich people" is not very
encouraging. First, he invites them to **"weep and cry aloud"** because of the
misery that is coming to them. That's an encouraging start, isn't it! Then, he
lists their offenses, the reasons they are facing this misery. These are the
same things that I mentioned earlier, but I want to look at them again a little
more closely; now that we know James might be talking to us, perhaps we're
all paying a bit more attention now!

There are four charges that James lays against the rich, but they fall
into two basic categories. The first is their personal use of money. James
starts by saying that they hoard their wealth, storing it up instead of using it
for others. The picture James paints here is really quite striking. In the first
century, wealth came in basically three forms: grain, gold or silver and fancy
clothes. Notice that James touches on each of these in verses 2 – 3. Their
wealth has rotted, because the grain they stored away was kept too long; it
has gone bad and is now worthless. Moths have eaten their clothes; note that
moths don't generally eat clothes that are being worn, so these are people
who have more clothes than they are able to wear, and the ones hanging in
the closet are getting ruined by moths; their wealth is literally being eaten
away. And their gold and silver has corroded. The word James uses here
actually means "rusted" which, of course, can't literally happen to gold or
silver, but I think the point is still clear: their wealth has been laying around
in storage for so long that even the gold is getting rusty. It has become
worthless, though perhaps the implication is that it is as good as worthless,
because the rich person refuses to ever spend it.

I can't help but see, in this passage, a reflection of Christ's words,
recorded in Matthew 6: 19 – 20: **"Do not accumulate for yourselves
treasures on earth, where moth and rust destroy and where thieves
break in and steal. But accumulate for yourselves treasures in heaven,
where moth and rust do not destroy, and thieves do not break in and
steal."** And that is, I think, really the problem. Not that these people are
wealthy but rather, that they are hoarding their wealth, storing up treasures

here on earth so that they can rely on themselves for their future, rather than trusting in God's provision in their lives.

And closely related to hoarding is the charge that they spend their wealth on luxurious living. James uses two interesting words here.[45] The first word, translated as "self-indulgence" means simply to live luxuriously. What I find interesting about this word is that, though it can refer to a life of sinful pleasure, it doesn't necessarily. It can (and often did) refer to innocent pleasures that have become the focus of one's life. So this luxurious living doesn't necessarily refer to a wild life of sin and debauchery; this could just as easily refer to any innocent pleasure (like taking walks or reading books) which has become the sole focus of a person's life. The second word, translated as "luxury" or "pleasure" has the connotation of one who lives solely for enjoyment, and one whose life of leisure is supported by the hard work of others; other people slave away so that this person can play. So the rich person James is speaking of hoards their wealth and only spends it to satisfy their desires, living a selfish life that is focused on ease and luxury.

The second category of charges James lists refers to how their use of wealth hurts others. First, James highlights how they keep their wealth from others by refusing to pay their workers. As he clearly states in verse 4: **"Look, the pay you have held back from the workers who mowed your fields cries out against you, and the cries of the reapers have reached the ears of the Lord of hosts."** So not only are these people hoarding their wealth, they also cheat their workers out of their fair pay. Adam Clarke points out that this was a situation that was particularly troubling to God.[46] There are two specific laws concerning paying laborers in the Old Testament: Leviticus 19:30 and Deuteronomy 24:15. Both of them say essentially the same thing: pay your workers before the sun goes down, lest they cry out to God against you and it become sin. The people James is describing here are flagrantly ignoring this law. Not only are they not paying their workers on the day the work was done, they're not paying their workers at all! According to Warren Wiersbe, the tense of the verb James uses here implies that these workers are never going to see their wages.

And notice the reaction of the workers. They cry out to the Lord. The name of God that James uses here is *Kurios Sabaoth*, the Lord of the Sabbath, or the Lord of Hosts. This is the name that signifies God's irresistible power and His position as the commander of the armies of Heaven. It was a name often used in the Old Testament; when Israel was threatened by foreign invaders, they would cry out to the Lord of Hosts and He would protect them. But here, it is the rich who are the oppressors, and the Lord of Hosts is about to step up to protect His people once again.

Finally, the rich use the power that their wealth gives them to oppress others. This explains why the workers didn't take their rich masters to court for their wages: wealth and power, in those days, made circumventing justice very easy. Judges would often accept bribes to "fix" cases, and even when bribes weren't given, judges were more likely to try to curry favor with the rich by ruling in their favor against the poor. So when the workers were cheated, the rich man's wealth shielded him from the consequences, thus their wealth was the primary tool used to deny justice to the poor.

Though this picture is likely intended to be read metaphorically, as with most of the pictures James paints for us in this epistle, I think it is important to note the emphatic language that he uses here in verse six: "**You have condemned and murdered the righteous person**." By circumventing justice, the rich people that James is condemning in this passage have figuratively, and perhaps literally, committed murder; not only that, they have killed innocent men, people who were righteous.

So James gives us a picture of a rich person who is slowly sinking deeper into sin because of their wealth. They are hoarding their wealth, counting on that as their future security but at the same time, they want to live a life of indulgence. So they begin to cheat their workers, spending what they should have paid in wages on their own luxuries, then using the influence that their wealth affords to make certain that the courts do not give their workers justice.

Not a very pretty picture, indeed.

The Fate of The Rich
But James takes this one step further; not only does he list the sins that these rich people have committed, he also describes for us their fate. First of all, the wealth that they have hoarded will testify against them when they stand before God. The irony here is priceless! They hoarded their wealth, thinking that it would protect them in their future. But in reality, it is their hoarded wealth that will speak up to condemn them.

And not only that; their hoarded wealth will also "**consume [their] flesh like fire**." The commentaries had a field day with this phrase. They had all sorts of theories about what exactly this might mean, though only one of them actually admitted that we really don't know. One thing I think we can say for certain: this doesn't sound like a good thing! And it seems to me to imply that not only will their hoarded wealth testify against them, but that wealth will also play a central part in the misery that awaits them as a punishment for their sins.

But the final judgment that James lists is, I think, the most eloquent: **"You have fattened your hearts in a day of slaughter."** The image being painted here is, I think, pretty clear: James is comparing these rich people to cattle that live lives of luxurious ease. They stand around in their stalls all day and do nothing but eat the choicest foods which are provided for them without any cost or labor on their part. That is how these rich people have lived their lives. But the cattle who were being fattened lived at ease so that they could be killed; their luxury marked them as destined for slaughter. And so it is, James seems to be saying, with these rich people. Their lives of luxury mark them as destined for destruction in the end.

There Your Heart Will Be Also

So where does all of this leave us? The first thing that I think we have to remember is that we are rich. God promises to give His people everything they need, and I can testify to how faithfully He has kept that promise to me and my family over the years of our ministry; chances are you can make the same testimony about your own experience. The thing is, before I started investigating this passage, that always seemed like a good thing, that I could confidently assert that God has always provided for all my needs. Now I'm not so sure. Because that confident assurance makes me rich, which means that I need to examine this passage carefully, to see if James is describing me.

But we don't really have to worry about that, do we? I mean, the person James describes in these verses is despicable! They are trusting in their wealth to provide their future security, they seem to be totally addicted to pleasure, and these desires have led them to cheat others and to oppress the poor. Surely that's not me! Surely none of you fall into that category, right?

The trouble is, the motivation of this rich person that James describes can be boiled down to two simple ideas. He wants to be able trust in himself, in his own wealth, rather than trusting in the provision of God. And, he wants to be comfortable, so he hoards and jealously guards what God has given him when he should be spending it on furthering God's Kingdom; he spends on himself what ought to have been given to meet the needs of others.

You see, essentially the problem is one of focus. God has provided abundantly, that this rich person might be an abundant blessing to those around him, thus drawing others into the light of God's Kingdom. But instead, he focused on the gift, not the Giver. He became enamored with the comfort and security that wealth brings and started to pursue wealth instead of pursing how he could use that wealth for God's glory. And in so doing, he incurred some hefty punishments.

I don't know about you, but one message that I take away from this passage is that God doesn't take it lightly when we waste the resources He's entrusted to us. When His stewards hoard or selfishly waste what He provides, God is not amused, and there are serious consequences.

I would encourage you to take some time right now to examine your heart and your life. How do you use the resources, the wealth, that God has entrusted to you? I think it is very easy, particularly when we are surrounded by today's Western culture, for us to flirt with materialism, to accommodate that little voice in our heads that says, "It's alright to spend this money on yourself. You deserve this!" Or that voice that says, "Don't give that money away! That poor person in front of you might need it, but if you give it away, you might not have enough for yourself!"

A better question to ask yourself is this: What is precious to you? What things in your life would you refuse to give up? In the movie *Leap Year*, a rather self-centered young woman is challenged with the question: "If your apartment was on fire and you had time to grab one thing to save it from the fire, what would that one thing be?" That is, in one sense, the question James is encouraging us to ask in this passage: If you could save one thing in your life, what would that thing be?

Or, to put it in the words of Christ, where is your heart? Because that is where you are laying up treasure, and if it isn't in the Kingdom of God, then likely you are simply fattening your heart for the day of slaughter.

I would encourage you to take a few minutes right now, prayerfully examining your heart. Ask God to show you the areas of your life where you have been hoarding His resources instead of spending them on His Kingdom, those places where you have set your heart on the things of this world and are storing up earthly treasures. Ask Him to help you let go of those things, that you might focus your whole heart and mind and all that you have, all that He has entrusted to you, on furthering the Kingdom of God.

Chapter Eighteen: Be Patient in Suffering

James 5: 7 – 12

**So be patient, brothers and sisters, until the
Lord's return. Think of how the farmer waits for the
precious fruit of the ground and is patient for it until it
receives the early and late rains. You also be patient and
strengthen your hearts, for the Lord's return is near. Do
not grumble against one another, brothers and sisters, so
that you may not be judged. See, the judge stands before
the gates! As an example of suffering and patience,
brothers and sisters, take the prophets who spoke in the
Lord's name. Think of how we regard as blessed those who
have endured. You have heard of Job's endurance and you
have seen the Lord's purpose, that the Lord is full of
compassion and mercy. And above all, my brothers and
sisters, do not swear, either by heaven or by earth or by
any other oath. But let your "Yes" be yes and your "No"
be no, so that you may not fall into judgment.**

It is axiomatic that, when you set yourself to speak or write on
patience or perseverance, the circumstances of your life as you prepare that
message will inevitably require the exercise of those virtues. So it was with
great trepidation that I originally came to this passage from James 5, and that
expectation was, sadly, not disappointed. That was a very long, difficult week
in my life, and the struggles of the week kept me from even working on the
message until the day before I was scheduled to give it in church, which
doesn't generally inspire me to feel greatly prepared or confident in speaking!
I'm starting this chapter now in another difficult season of life, and it makes
me wonder what else is looming ahead that will help give me the chance to
practice the virtues James highlights for us in this passage.

But it strikes me that some teaching on the topic of patience in
suffering is probably always timely; remember James taught us in chapter 1
to expect trials and temptations as a normal part of our Christian experience.
That's part of what the Christian life here on earth is about. So I suspect that
there are many of you reading this today who are struggling with difficulties

of various kinds in your life. Maybe you, like me, are very curious to discover exactly what James has to say to us about patience as we endure suffering.

Be Patient

And of course, as always, I start out with the words of the passage. I wanted to know, first of all, exactly what James meant when he counseled us to be patient. Obviously, this is an important idea in this passage; James expresses this concept, variously translated as "patience" or "endurance," five times in these five verses, twice in verse 7 and once each in verses 8, 10 and 11. And he uses two different Greek words to express these concepts. The first one, *makrothumeo,* which is most often translated as "patience," means "to be of a long spirit, not to lose heart" or "to persevere patiently and bravely in enduring misfortunes and troubles." The second one, used only in verse 11, is *hupomone,* which means "steadfastness, constancy, endurance." But in practice, this word meant, "the characteristic of a man who is not swerved from his deliberate purpose and his loyalty to faith and piety by even the greatest trials and sufferings." I like the way that Charles Tyree summarizes these two ideas: "They can be synonyms, but here, the first word implies 'patient waiting' and the second 'fortitude,' the strength that comes from patience." So in essence, James is counseling us to patiently wait on the Lord, so that we can, in the process, be strengthened.

But, to complement these precise words, James also gives us three examples of the kind of patience he is encouraging believers to practice. The first is the example of the farmer. In some ways, this is the perfect example of a patience that is born of faith. Each year, the farmer plants his crops in the hopeful expectation of a harvest at the end of the season. So many things could intervene and destroy that harvest. Animals could come eat the plants before they are ready. Insects or disease could destroy them. Too much rain might make them rot. Too little rain might dry them out and kill them. These things are, for the most part, beyond the farmer's control. But still he plants and faithfully toils over his fields, in anticipation of the eventual harvest.

So the farmer believes that the harvest will come, that God will add His blessing and protection to the farmer's labor. And the farmer is willing to wait for his labor to come to fruition. As Warren Weiresbe puts it, "If a man is impatient, he had better not become a farmer," because farmers have to wait a long time before they see any fruit from their labor; as Tyree rather whimsically points out, "No amount of begging or pleading or the threat of force [will] make a garden grow any faster." If a farmer wants to enjoy the fruit of the harvest, he has to patiently wait for it to come.

So in essence, the first exhortation James gives in this passage is that we are to be like spiritual farmers. Just as a farmer patiently waits for God to provide a harvest of grain, we should wait patiently for God to take the difficult circumstances of our lives and create from them a bountiful harvest of spiritual fruit.

Then, in verse 10, James brings up his second example: the prophets. Of course, this was a very familiar topic for the Jews that were James' original audience. They were in the habit of gathering regularly in their synagogues, where they would read from the prophets. So undoubtedly, when James mentions the prophets as examples of patience in suffering, many different names came immediately to the readers' minds. You could pretty much list any one of them, because to be a prophet almost always meant to live a life of suffering for the Lord's sake.

As examples of patience, the prophets demonstrate several different principles. First, the prophets were living according to God's will and they still experienced suffering. Many people have the idea that suffering is always the result of sin in our lives, which would mean that when we are right with God, living righteously, all should be well in our lives. Of course, nothing could be further from the reality of the Christian life. In fact, based on the example of the prophets, it would seem that sometimes we experience suffering *because* we are living according to God's will. Which is not to say, of course, that sin is never a factor; we should always examine our hearts to make sure that the difficulties we are facing are not stemming from unconfessed sin in our lives. But here, James reminds us that sometimes, suffering comes not because we have sinned, but rather because we are standing up and living for God.

Secondly, the suffering of the prophets reminds us that God is always with us, even in the midst of suffering. Elijah is a great example of this. God led him to pray for a drought that lasted three years. During that time of drought, God directed him to live in the perfect place. It was protected, so King Ahab wouldn't find him and there was a reliable source of water for him to use. And, if that wasn't enough, God sent ravens every day to feed him. Even in the midst of drought and persecution, God took care of all of

Elijah's needs. We can expect the same kind of care in the midst of our suffering; well, maybe without the ravens, but He will provide all that we need, even in, especially in, the midst of difficult circumstances.

Finally, the suffering of the prophets allowed their lives to be a greater witness to those around them, or, as Wiersbe puts it, "that their lives might back up their messages." James knew that in the midst of suffering and difficult circumstances, it is easy for people to get discouraged and loose heart. But the example of someone who endured suffering and survived with their faith intact can be a powerful encouragement. And that's not only true of the prophets. Just as the lives of the prophets can be an encouragement in our lives, so the suffering that we patiently endure can be an encouragement in the lives of those around us.

In all of these ways, and undoubtedly in many others, the lives of the prophets are a great illustration of what it means to patiently endure in the face of suffering.

And then, James gives us his final example of patience: the life of Job. Of course, Job is the epitome of patiently enduring in the face of suffering. Chances are we all know the story. He was a powerful, wealthy man and then, through no fault of his own, he lost everything: his wealth, his children, his health, his reputation. And still, even in the midst of all of this suffering, he refused to sin by complaining against God.

Certainly there are many lessons we can learn from the life of Job (maybe I'll do my next commentary on that book!), but Wiersbe points out one lesson that I think is worth noting here. When we are in the midst of suffering that is undeserved, Satan will often encourage us to try to get out of it, to try to end the suffering in our own way or in our own strength. Wiersbe suggests that following this impulse is essentially impatience. For example, Abraham became impatient for God to fulfill His promise of a son, so, at the urging of Sarah, he tried to help God along. The result was Ishmael, whose descendents have become the mortal enemies of the Jews. How different might the world be today if Abraham had been patient in waiting for the Lord's timing!

So, in this example of Job, James is encouraging us to patiently wait for God's perfect timing and to trust in His grace to sustain us in times of trouble. The example of this that Wiersbe points out is Paul, who speaks of a thorn in his flesh, which he describes in 2 Corinthians as **"a messenger of Satan."** Though he pleads with God to remove it, God simply replies, **"My**

grace is enough for you." And rather than fighting this answer or seeking his own remedy, his own way out, instead Paul responds, "**So then, I will boast most gladly about my weaknesses, so that the power of Christ may reside in me.**" The same grace that sustained Paul is available to us; all we have to do is ask.

Taking these three examples together, what can we say about the patience James encourages believers to demonstrate? I think Wiersbe sums it up very well:

> James wanted to encourage us to be patient in times of suffering. Like the farmer, we are waiting for a spiritual harvest, for fruit that will glorify God. Like the prophets, we look for opportunities for witness, to share the truth of God. And, like Job, we wait for the Lord to fulfill His loving purpose.

Grumbling and Swearing

But in the midst of these verses describing patience in suffering, James throws in verse 9 and verse 12, neither one of which seem to have much of anything to do with the topic at hand. In verse 9, James admonishes the believers not to grumble against each other, and verse 12 talks about not swearing. Where did these two verses come from? What is James trying to do here?

Tyree explains verse 9 this way: When people are in pain, when they are suffering, the natural reaction is to complain. And we tend to complain against whoever is nearby, regardless of whether or not they are responsible for our suffering. Nurses often take the brunt of our grumbling, not because they cause our pain, but because they are there while we are in pain. We can't grumble at the disease or injury we're suffering, so we grumble against the one who is there to help us. And the church sometimes functions in the same way. When believers are experiencing difficult circumstances, their natural reaction is to complain. They can't grumble against God (or if they do, it doesn't make them feel any better), so they grumble against those who are around them: other believers.

So in the midst of his admonition to patiently bear suffering, James includes this caveat about how we should treat our fellow believers while we are patiently bearing suffering: don't grumble against each other! Though I like the way Wiersbe puts it the best: "Impatience with God often leads to impatience with God's people, and this is a sin we must avoid. If we [spiritual farmers] start using [our] sickles on each other, we will miss the harvest!"

Wiersbe also has a good explanation for verse 12. He suggests that when experiencing suffering, it is very easy for us to say anything that we think might help relieve that suffering. I'm reminded here of the famous saying that there are no atheists in foxholes. There is a good example of this in an episode of the old tv show MASH. Father Mulcahy, the company priest, is called over to a recovering soldier's hospital bed, where the soldier confesses that, in the middle of the battle in which he was wounded, he made a deal with God. He promised that if God would rescue him from the battle, then he would become a priest. God did His part and rescued the soldier, but now, the soldier doesn't want to become a priest. Father Mulcahy chuckles at this story and responds that if everyone who made such a promise followed through with it, there would be more priests than parishioners. In essence, Mulcahy tells the soldier that it is okay to go back on his promise to God, that God won't hold him to what he promised in the midst of such difficult circumstances.

Unfortunately, James seems to indicate that Father Mulcahy may have gotten it wrong. God does, indeed, care about what we say, and He expects us to keep our oaths, no matter what the circumstances, even if we make them in the midst of suffering. So, James tells us, the solution is not to swear. Just say "yes" or "no" and let it go at that. In that way, you will avoid condemnation.

And when you think about it, that makes perfect sense. If you are living a life of integrity, guarding carefully the words that come out of your mouth, then you shouldn't ever need oaths to make people believe what you say; a person of with a reputation for integrity doesn't need an oath to convince people that they are trustworthy; just a simple "yes" or "no" will do.

Why Should We Be Patient?

So, James calls us to be patient in suffering and gives us some examples of people who have done just that, to encourage us on our way. But what I think is most important is the reason he holds up for us. Why should we patiently bear suffering? **Because the Lord's return is near. Because the judge stands before the gates**! For anyone who is dwelling in sin, that would be a rather ominous image, wouldn't it? Tyree tells a story about how he and his brother used to carry on in their room at night after their father had told them to be quiet. They would enjoy themselves, talking and playing, until they heard their father's footsteps approaching the door for the second time. When they knew he was there, just on the other side of the door, when discipline was only a step away, suddenly obedience became much more attractive! And I think pretty much every parent has experienced this reality. I can't tell you how many times, over the years, I have asked my children to stop doing something, only to watch them stop for a moment and then continue doing what they were doing. This pattern would continue until I got up and approached the child. At that point, they knew discipline was coming; they had pushed the limit too far and now they were in for it. Invariably, as I approached, suddenly the child became the model son or daughter, sitting and doing exactly what I had earlier commanded them to do. Judgment was coming, and they were suddenly very motivated to obey!

But to the oppressed, to those who are suffering for righteousness sake, the approach of the Judge is cause for great celebration. Yes, we are oppressed and downtrodden now, but just wait! The Judge is coming! He is right outside the door, and very soon, He is going to come in and make everything right! That is the hope that James held out to these first century Jewish believers. They were outcasts of society, shunned and hated by almost everyone outside of the church, and many of them were suffering greatly for their faith, suffering in ways that we, today, can scarcely imagine. But they lived in the expectation that soon, Christ would return, and He would right all the wrongs. As the Righteous Judge, He would vindicate them.

What I find most encouraging about this is that we live with that same hopeful expectation today. The first century church believed they would see Christ's return; they consciously looked at each day as one day closer to His coming. Well, His coming is a lot closer now than it was then. In fact, it is closer now than it was when you started reading this chapter.

The Righteous Judge is coming, and coming soon. So be patient and endure the suffering that you must face today. Don't take your frustration out on the believers around you and don't speak foolishly, making oaths that you don't really mean. Be encouraged by the examples God has given us, and keep working to bring in the harvest until the Day comes, and He arrives to bring us all Home.

Because the Day of the Lord is drawing near!

James 5: 13 – 18

Is anyone among you suffering? He should pray. Is anyone in good spirits? He should sing praises. Is anyone among you ill? He should summon the elders of the church, and they should pray for him and anoint him with oil in the name of the Lord. And the prayer of faith will save the one who is sick and the Lord will raise him up – and if he has committed sins, he will be forgiven. So confess your sins to one another and pray for one another so that you may be healed. The prayer of a righteous person has great effectiveness. Elijah was a human being like us, and he prayed earnestly that it would not rain and there was no rain on the land for three years and six months! Then he prayed again, and the sky gave rain and the land sprouted with a harvest.

Charles Tyree tells a story of a pastor who was trying to help a member of his congregation. This man came to the pastor and began pouring out his heart, sharing a long list of all the troubles and difficulties that he was struggling with in his life at that time. And as he finished listing all of these struggles, he blurted out, "I'm in real trouble here, so don't just tell me to pray!"

Do you ever have that attitude about prayer? Do you ever find yourself looking at prayer that way, as something that it is good to do, that we ought to do as Christians, but something that really has no practical value? If you're like me, when the need is serious, we want to be doing something real, not just praying.

There were some folks who worked with us here in Cameroon several years ago named Bill and Wendy Myers. At one point, Wendy came down with a serious case of malaria. This was a *really* bad case, so bad, in fact, that the technicians who tested her blood at the lab wanted to know why they were testing blood from a corpse; the malaria count was so high, they couldn't believe that the person was still alive! And she was very close to death; her family and the missionary community here were all preparing for the worst. And I remember struggling with feeling utterly powerless. There was absolutely nothing I could do to help the situation; all I could do was pray. And I'm afraid I meant that in the worst sense of that expression: practically speaking, I felt like I couldn't do anything at all.

I don't know about you, but I often struggle with this idea, with the feeling that prayer is an important, personal spiritual exercise, or a serious Christian duty, but generally speaking it is of no practical use. Unless you are a super-Christian, card carrying member of the Move Mountains Club, prayer really doesn't do anything. James has a clear and powerful answer to that idea in the passage we are focusing on in this chapter; let's walk through verses 13 – 18 of chapter 5 to see what James has to teach us about prayer.

The Realms of Prayer

Tyree points out that the first half of this passage highlights several realms or areas of prayer that ought to be present in a mature believer's life. The first of these is the realm of personal prayer. **"Is anyone among you suffering?"** James asks. And the answer is, **"He should pray."** The Greek word James uses for "suffering" means "to suffer hardship." It was a fairly common word and referred to any kind of hardship or misfortune. Not just the huge, life changing or life threatening needs, but also the "stub your toe", "please don't let it rain" variety of needs. So basically James is asking, "Do you have any kind of problem in your life?" Which, in the context that James was writing in, was a particularly silly question to ask. Remember, his audience was first century Jewish Christians, people who were rejected by everyone in society. The Romans hated them because they were Jews; the Jews hated them because they were Christians. They were discriminated against from every side, and many of them were very poor. Not only that, but because of their faith, they could be arrested, attacked or killed pretty much at any time. Life was *hard* for these people.

And in response to these troubles, great and small, James says, "Pray."

One of the things that spoke to me in this verse was the inclusiveness of the word James uses for "suffering." God is not only interested in hearing about the huge problems of our lives; there is no "severity threshold" that our problems have to surpass in order for them to qualify as a prayer request. No, God wants to hear about all the things that trouble us; He wants us to turn to Him in every circumstance.

And that includes times of joy as well, as the second half of verse 13 clarifies: **"Is anyone in good spirits? He should sing praises."** The word translated here as "good spirits" in the Greek literally means "to have the mind well," which implies this is not the superficial happiness that comes from the lack of difficult circumstances. Rather, this is the deep joy of believers who are resting contentedly on their faith in God.

So James is writing to people on both ends of the spectrum: people who are suffering and struggling with their problems as well as people who have found contentment and joy that transcends their current circumstances; people who are living in the joy of the Lord, as Scripture frequently describes it. But what really strikes me here is that, no matter where you fall on this spectrum, the response is the same: turn to God. When you are struggling, turn to Him in prayer. When you are joyful, turn to Him in praise. No matter what our circumstances, our focus should be God-ward, turning our eyes to Him in supplication or in praise.

But then, in verse 14, James expands the sphere of personal prayer to include prayer for illness or disease. **"Is anyone among you ill? He should summon the elders of the church, and they should pray for him and anoint him with oil in the name of the Lord."** Now, I have to say that this is another one of those passages that I find rather troubling. Apparently I'm not alone in that either; many of the commentaries I read pretty much just skipped over verse 14; they were far more interested in explaining what James meant in verse 15: **"And the prayer of faith will save the one who is sick and the Lord will raise him up."** Or perhaps more precisely, these commentators were anxious to explain what verse 15 does not mean. A fairly reasonable response, I have to admit, because if this verse is taken literally, then James is saying here that whenever we get sick, all we need to do is call the Elders of the church to pray for us and we will always be healed. Clearly that is not true. We don't even need to turn to the record of Scripture to prove that (though we could); I would venture to say that all of us, in our own experience, have known times or circumstances where we prayed for healing but healing never came. So obviously James is not lifting up the prayers of the church Elders as some kind of magic formula that is guaranteed to cure all your physical problems!

But of course, if that isn't what James is saying here, the question remains, what *is* he trying to say? Well, there are two details that I want to point out which I hope will shed some light on that question. First, in verse 14, James says the sick person should call for the Elders of the church to pray over him. Tyree points out that the verb tense James uses here makes this an urgent command. In other words, James is saying that before you do anything else, call for prayer. And who should we call on? The Elders of the church. Now, being an Elder in the international church here in Yaoundé, this made me a little bit nervous, so I looked up the Greek word that James uses here for "elders," hoping, I have to admit, that it meant something generic, referring simply to mature believers or something like that. No such luck; the word used here is the one used exclusively in the New Testament to refer to the leaders of the church. When Paul founded a church, he left elders, or *presbuteros* (from which the English word presbyters comes), in charge. That is who James is referring to here: the leaders of the church. Of course, this does not mean that no one else is allowed to pray for the sick to be healed. Scripture clearly calls all believers to lift all of their cares and concerns up to the Lord, and that would certainly include concerns about health. It would be foolish to imagine that this verse is meant to be restrictive.

But, on the other hand, James does seem to be saying that those who have been called to be leaders of the church have a particular obligation to minister in prayer to the sick, which is why I was rather hoping to discover that the word actually meant something else. As one of the leaders in my church, I'm not particularly comfortable with the thought of everyone in the church (and we're not a very big church) coming to me and asking for healing; I'm pretty sure that I'm not feeling up to that responsibility! I feel like I should quickly add that I would never refuse such a request, if it was made; I just don't feel particularly qualified to minister to others in healing prayer.

And I think at least part of my hesitation in this regard comes from the second point that I want to mention about this section. Verse 15 has a very interesting phrase: "**the prayer of faith**." The commentaries had many opinions as to what, exactly James meant by this phrase, though I think the one that makes most sense was in the King James Study Bible, which said, "The prayer of faith discerns God's will and perseveres until it is accomplished. God's will, however, is not to heal in every case, and true faith can *discern* and *accept* that." In other words, the implication is that the Elders who are being called on to pray for the sick are actively and earnestly seeking God's will in the situation. Not only that, they are also spiritually mature enough to be able to discern the leading of God's Spirit. So they are confident that their prayers for the sick will be answered with healing, because they are praying as Christ did, according to the Father's will.

But I think the critical idea in this passage is, again, the focus. We should call the elders, who should pray in faith, but in the end, it is the Lord who will raise the sick person up, the Lord who will heal them. And that is important to understand and clearly remember. The focus is not on who we call to pray nor on how great their faith is. It is certainly not about the ritual we go through when we pray; details like what kind of oil we use or whether we use oil at all really don't make a bit of difference. The focus is on God. He is the one who heals us, when we turn our eyes to Him in faith.

Then, in the end of verse 15 and through verse 16, James expands the sphere of prayer again. We are also to pray together for the forgiveness of our sins. Or, as James puts it, **"if [the sick person] has committed sins, he will be forgiven. So confess your sins to one another and pray for one another so that you may be healed. The prayer of a righteous person has great effectiveness."** Now, once again I have to admit that I was tempted to just quickly gloss over this verse; many of the commentaries contented themselves with acknowledging that this is a difficult verse to sort out before heading on to verse 17. At the start, James seems to be implying that the sick person who needs prayer from the Elders needs that prayer because their illness was caused by sin; in fact, some commentaries were quite confident that the prayer James describes here only applies to sickness that is caused by sin. Then, James seems to tell us to share all of our sins together, so that we can pray for each other. That would imply that our church services ought to include an open microphone confession time, right before prayer time, so that everyone who has sinned during the week can come up and publicly confess those sins and be prayed for. Does that sound like a good idea to you?

Of course, I can't say that I know for certain what James means in this verse, but I do have a few ideas that I'd like to point out. First, as many commentaries were quick to point out, confession in this verse is not to the priest or the elders; we are to confess our sins to each other, to the body of the church. I'm not going to speculate too long on how public these confessions need to be, because James doesn't say. I do think, however, that a good general principle is that the confession should be as private as the sin; the more public the effect of the sin, the more public the confession ought to be.

But more important than who we are confessing to is why we are confessing. James gives us two reasons: that the church can lift us up in prayer and so that we can be healed. It is worth noting that the word for "healed" that James uses here is different from the one he used in verse 15; in this case, the word literally means "to make whole," and the implication is that this is a spiritual healing. And that brings out, once again, the God-ward focus that runs all through this passage. Why should we confess our sins and pray for one another? So that we can be healed spiritually and made right with God.

The Righteous Person's Prayer

So James highlights three spheres of prayer that a mature Christian ought to have in their life; three ways that a mature believer ought to be praying. There is personal prayer, both in supplication for our needs and prayers of thanksgiving and praise; there is prayer for healing of our physical infirmities; and there is prayer for spiritual healing. And then, in the second half of this passage, he lifts up an example for us to follow on this journey of prayer.

And I need to admit right at the start that I was rather disappointed by his choice: Elijah. Seems to me that he sets the bar pretty high. Couldn't he have started out with someone more at my level, like maybe Lot? Of course, the point is that Elijah was not a superman; he was a normal person, just like us. He fled in fear before the threats of Jezebel; he struggled with doubt and loneliness to the point of begging God to just kill him. And yet, in spite of that, look what he did! He prayed and the rain stopped for three and a half years. Then, he prayed again and the rain returned. Not to mention, in between those prayers, he had a little altercation with the prophets of Baal on Mount Carmel.

And he accomplished all of these amazing feats of faith not because he was supernaturally gifted with uncommon faith. No, it was all because he was listening to God. Because he knew God's voice, he knew what God was calling him to do, so he could pray in perfect faith, completely confident that he was asking what God wanted him to ask, completely confident that his prayers would be answered.

And if there is one idea that I have taken away from my study of this passage, it would be that. When we are standing in God's will, when we are listening to Him and learning to desire what He desires for our lives, then our prayers matter. Or, as James puts it, **"The prayer of a righteous person has**

great effectiveness.”

I think it is easy for us to forget how powerful prayer can be, because we can't always see the immediate effects of our prayers, so it is easy to begin viewing prayer as simply a meaningless religious exercise. And when our focus in prayer is on ourselves, when we are focused on our own needs, our own desires, our own will, then I would suggest that it really is basically a meaningless exercise. As long as our focus is on ourselves, we can have no real confidence that our prayers will make a difference. Don't misunderstand me here; I'm not suggesting that such prayers will not be heard. God has promised that He is always listening to the prayers of His people. But when we are focused on what we want, how can we be sure that we are praying for what God wants? Elijah could pray confidently that it would not rain because he knew God's will was for Israel to have a drought. If I was to pray that prayer today, I wouldn't be nearly that confident, and I bet my results wouldn't be nearly as spectacular.

The key, as James shows us in this passage, is our focus on God. As we abide in Him, as we grow close to Him and know Him better, as we seek to make His will our own, then we can have confidence that our prayers will be asking for what He wants. As you pray for needs in your own life, as you pray for those around you who are sick, as you pray for the spiritual vitality of your local church body, be actively seeking His will; be abiding in Him.

So that your prayers might have great effectiveness.

Chapter Twenty: Take Care of Each Other

James 5: 19 – 20

> **My brothers and sisters, if anyone among you wanders from the truth and someone turns him back, he should know that the one who turns a sinner back from his wandering path will save that person's soul from death and will cover a multitude of sins.**

I think it is pretty safe to say the C. S. Lewis is my favorite Christian author. There is very little that Lewis has written that I haven't read, and almost all of it I thoroughly enjoy; maybe some of you will agree with me on that score. However, there is one thing about his writing that has always rather bothered me: his conclusions. Now, I'm not talking primarily about his fiction; in general, his stories end quite well. But in his non-fiction, his essays and theological works, often his conclusions are painfully brief; sometimes they're not even there at all. In many cases, it seems like he just stopped writing and walked away; maybe he headed out for a cup of tea and when he got back to his desk, he forgot that he hadn't finished and sent the essay in to his publisher as it was. This tendency of his has always greatly bothered me. If he was writing in one of my classes, I would put brackets around his final paragraphs and make snide comments about abrupt endings or running out of time.

And I find myself having the same reaction to the end of the epistle of James. He has been charging along in chapter 5, giving advice and teaching on a fairly wide variety of issues, though all focused on the same general topic that he has been addressing in the entire letter: What does it mean to live a genuine, mature Christian life? Then, we come to verses 19 – 20, a quick statement about accountability, and that's all we get; that is the end of the letter. It rather reminds me of some of the in class essays that my AP English Language students write. They'll be writing along, doing just fine and then, suddenly they realize they only have five minutes left. So, they panic and frantically try to cram everything else that they have to say into the last three sentences before throwing on a hasty conclusion.

That's what the entire second half of chapter 5 feels like to me. It is as if James suddenly realized he was running out of parchment so he just started firing off all the final bits of instruction that he was hoping to get into the letter. But he can't quite fit it all in. I can almost picture him continuing to dictate more of the letter after verse 20, when his scribe sheepishly stops him saying, "Um, James, sorry but I'm out of parchment. We don't have any more space." And James thinks about it for a minute, then replies, "Oh well, just send it like that, then."

A rather absurd picture, but one that is close to the fear that many scholars have in connection with this epistle. The ending is so abrupt that some commentators have suggested that there was originally more to the letter and what we have in the Bible today is actually just a fragment of what James originally wrote. Of course, they were quick to insist (and rightly, I might add), that God gave us all of the letter that we require; they were not suggesting that we're missing some important theological truth that, if it was to be suddenly revealed, would change our understanding of Christ or Christian living. No, we might not have the whole letter, but we're not missing anything crucial, anything that we absolutely needed to hear.

Though I have to admit that the abruptness of these final two verses made me hesitate to write the message on which this chapter is based. When I got to these verses during my original sermon series on James, I was, at first, tempted to just tack them onto the end of the last passage, which we discussed together in the last chapter. Unfortunately, they just didn't fit in well enough with verses 13 – 18, so I couldn't find a way to incorporate them into that message. Failing that, I was tempted to just ignore them. I mean, it is only two verses, one full sentence. And it basically just says what it says; no need for deep interpretation or explication here, I thought. So was it really worth the effort, for the space of a whole message (or a whole chapter, for that matter), to dwell on these final two verses?

Chances are, since you are still reading this, you've figured out what my answer to that question ultimately was. Of course, I feel it is only fair to admit that at least part of my decision was based on the fact that I wanted to finish what I had started. Since I am only called on to speak in church periodically (and rarely more frequently than once a month, often less than that) I originally spent three years working through this sermon series on the book of James at the International Christian Church of Yaoundé, and after all of that time, I just couldn't stand the thought of not finishing the entire book. But also, as I was originally in the midst of this decision, God reminded me of the familiar passage about Scripture found in 2 Timothy 3: "**Every scripture is inspired by God**." That means that these two verses, this one sentence, this final thought tacked on to the end of this epistle, originated in the mind of God. He felt it was worth preserving for us to read 2000 years after it was written; He felt it was useful for our teaching and edification.

Chances are, if God thinks these two verses were worth preserving, then they're worth our time to look at a little more closely; maybe, in this closing thought that James leaves us with, you will find something that is useful and encouraging in your walk with Christ.

Bring Them Back

4Now, the basic message of these verses deals with our duty to fellow believers, and I think there are a few details that are worth pointing out here. First, James addresses this final exhortation to all believers. The word he uses in verse 19 (appropriately translated by the NET as "brothers and sisters") is the generic term used throughout the New Testament to denote followers of Christ. So he is not talking just to the Elders or leaders of the church, as he does in verse 14; here, this exhortation is directed at all of us, at all believers.

Second, James refers here to one who has wandered away from the truth. Now, it is fairly clear that he is still speaking of Christians, someone who was or is a believer, a member of the church. What is, perhaps, a bit less clear is exactly what he means by the phrase, **"wanders from the truth."** The word James uses for "wander" is *planao*, which is another of those interesting Greek words that have a variety of meanings. The King James version translates it throughout the New Testament in various ways; as "deceive", "err", "go astray", "seduce" and "wander." In essence, it means to lead, or to be led, away from the truth into error, often with the implication of deceiving oneself. And, interestingly enough, when used with the definite article, it is a common title for the Devil: the Deceiver.

The point is, however, that this word covers pretty much any kind of error that a believer could possibly fall into, from a misunderstanding of Scripture that leads to false doctrine, to being led astray by false teaching, to willful disobedience – when you understand what you should do but then you go and do the opposite anyway. All of these kinds of errors are covered by this word, and I think James uses this very generic term intentionally. He did now want this exhortation to be limited to certain, specific circumstances; he didn't want people to imagine that he was referring to errors that only result from a particular circumstance or some particular sin. He wanted this to apply to all cases; any time a believer falls into any kind of error, for any reason, this exhortation applies.

And what, exactly, does James exhort us to do in these situations? Simple: bring them back. On one level, it doesn't get any more basic than that. This brother or sister has wandered away from the truth, so bring them back to the truth. I find it interesting that James does not proscribe how these erring believers ought to be brought back; again, he remains very general, which, to me, implies that we ought to use whatever means seem appropriate for each situation as we seek to bring our fellow believers back to the truth. That would include prayer; when you see someone who has wandered from the truth, lift them up in prayer. Pray that God would reveal their error to them and convict them of their sin, that they might return to the truth. It would also include confrontation; Paul lays out the process for confronting a brother or sister who is living in sin, and that process could also apply here. But the point is, we are to do whatever it takes, following the guidance of the Holy Spirit, to bring these brothers or sisters back.

One final idea that I think is worth mentioning about this verse is this: the way James phrases this verse implies that these wandering believers have done nothing to initiate the process of being brought back to the church. In other words, it is our job, as faithful believers, to seek them out. We can't wait for them to see the light and come back to us; we have to go get them. We have to meet them where they are, in the midst of their error, and work to bring them back to the truth. This is important to note because our tendency, I think, is to be more passive in this area. It is more comfortable for most of us to wait for them to come and ask for our help (and more affirming to our pride as well); in general, I think most people find it very uncomfortable, very daunting, to confront someone in this way. James doesn't really give us that option. He seems to assume that we will be actively pursuing these believers who have wandered from the truth.

To Cover Over Sin

And perhaps James has good reason to expect that we will be seeking out these lost believers: look at the rewards he lists in verse 20 for fulfilling this duty. He mentions two basic consequences. First, we will save a sinner from death and second, we will cover a multitude of sins.

The commentators that I read had a lot of trouble with this first consequence: saving a sinner from death. And unfortunately, the original Greek for this phrase isn't much help; the words James uses here simply mean "to save a sinner from death.' Not a lot of help there. So, the commentators spent a lot of time pondering and discussing the various possible issues that James might be raising here. Is he talking about physical or spiritual death? Does this verse imply that a believer, by wandering away from the truth, can lose their salvation?

But as far as I'm concerned, there is one implication that is far more significant than answering any of these questions. That is the fact that bringing wandering believers back to the truth is vitally important. The stakes involved here are very high. It doesn't really matter what kind of death James is referring to here; in any case, believers who have wandered away from the truth are in deadly danger. And according to James, God has ordained that we who remain faithful to the truth should be the instrument of their salvation, of their return to the truth.

Don't misunderstand me here; I'm not suggesting that God somehow needs our help, or that we somehow replace or add to the work of salvation that Christ accomplished on the cross. What He did was sufficient to cover all the sins of all mankind, and there is nothing that any of us can do to add anything to the salvation that is our free gift through faith in Jesus. What I do see James saying here is that God chooses to use us as His instruments of reconciliation in the lives of these wayward believers. He could just as easily choose someone or something else (remember the donkey he chose to use in rescuing Balaam back in Numbers?), but He desires to work through us. Make no mistake: His will is going to be done in the lives of these believers. The only question is whether we will receive the blessing that He designed for us by being faithful to this call to minister to believers who have gone astray.

The commentators were also rather troubled by the second part of verse 20: covering a multitude of sins. The biggest problem here was actually the grammar. The way James phrases this verse, it is unclear whose sins are being covered over. Thus, some groups have concluded that James is teaching that when we bring back a wayward believer, a multitude of our own sins are covered. This would, of course, have the obvious implication that we can find forgiveness for our sins (and thus, ultimately, salvation) through our own actions, through a vehicle other than the saving work of Christ on the cross.

The grammar of this verse allows for such an interpretation, but the teaching of Scripture as a whole clearly does not. So obviously, if we accept that this epistle is inspired by God and agrees with the rest of the teaching of

Scripture, this can't be what James is trying to say here. But the trouble is, if this phrase doesn't apply to the one doing the rescuing, it must apply to the one being rescued. In my mind, that makes this a rather weak reward for the rescuer. The person being brought back gets all the good stuff: their life is saved and their sins are covered over. The rescuer doesn't seem to get much out of the deal!

At least, that's true when you look at this from a worldly perspective. But I think the point is that we should be seeing it from God's perspective. His desire is that all people would turn to Him and be saved, but those who are in the church, His adopted sons and daughters are particularly precious to Him. Think of this relationship in human terms for a second. If I'm walking along the street and I see a child in danger, I would step in and try to help them; I wouldn't want harm to come to any child if I was able to prevent it. That impulse is behind those heroic stories of teachers who put themselves in harm's way in order to save the lives of their students; I think of people like Victoria Soto, a teacher at Newtown Elementary during the tragic shooting a few years ago; she hid her students and then faced down the gunman alone, losing her own life for the sake of saving her kids. As a teacher, I could see myself doing something like that. Probably. But if the child in harm's way was one of my own children, there is no "probably" about it; nothing would keep me from stepping out to protect them; no matter what it cost me, I would save them if I could. And I think the same is true of God; His desire is that none should perish, but when it is His children, His Church standing in peril, He is particularly concerned. He particularly desires for them to be rescued and restored.

Now, take that one step further. Imagine one of my own children was in deadly danger and I was in a position where I could go out and rescue them. What reward would I be looking for in that circumstance? It seems to me that the greatest reward I could have would be getting my kids to safety. I wouldn't be looking for fame or money or anything like that; those things would be meaningless compared to knowing my child is safe. That is the situation James is highlighting in this verse: from God's perspective, the reward is knowing that His child has been restored, His child is no longer in danger of death. And James seems to be implying that we ought to be looking at this situation from God's perspective. As we see this rescued believer through God's eyes, then we receive our reward: the knowledge that one of God's precious children, who was in grave, deadly danger, is now safe again.

So Take Care of One Another

There are undoubtedly many different lessons that can be drawn from these verses, but the one that strikes me is perhaps the most obvious of these: as believers, we are responsible for each other. Scripture calls us the Body of Christ, and in this passage, James seems to be calling us to act like it. When one of us is hurting, when one of us is wandering from the truth, thus putting their spiritual life in jeopardy, that ought to matter to us. In fact, it ought to matter enough to impel us to take action.

Of course, you could look at this from a fairly negative perspective if you want to. In that scenario, we within the church are all carefully watching each other for signs of error or moral lapse, and when we see those signs, we pounce. I'm fairly certain that is not the picture that James is trying to paint here, though. Instead, I think he is implying that we, as a church, ought to be engaged in each other's lives. We ought to be willing, on the one hand, to honestly share with other believers how we are doing; share what God is teaching us, share areas of our lives where we are struggling, share places that we need the support and prayers of our brothers and sisters in Christ. And, on the other hand, we ought to be willing to listen to each other. We should work to make sure we are not too busy or too wrapped up in our own lives that we can't take the time required to actually hear each other, to actually support one another.

So that, when people in our Body are struggling, when someone wanders away from the truth, for whatever reason, we not only notice but we take action; we seek them out and prayerfully, lovingly seek to bring them back, so that the Body of Christ might be whole once again.

Chapter Twenty-One: Final Thoughts

Congratulations! You've made it all the way to the end of these meandering musings on this epistle of James'. I appreciate you staying with me for this journey; I pray that you've found some encouragement in these pages to help you be more like Jesus in your day to day life.

This being the second commentary that I have written based on a series of sermons that I originally presented at the International Church of Yaoundé, I was anticipating the pleasure of walking through these messages again. And I was not disappointed; The book of James is a veritable treasure trove of practical wisdom for living a successful Christian life and I greatly enjoyed walking this road again, clarifying and expounding on points that I had originally made in these messages. There were many times when I was reminded of, and again convicted by, the truths that James has to share in his epistle.

However, as I have pondered, over the last few days, how I should conclude this commentary on the book of James, one thought keeps coming back to my mind: this is *hard*! James really sets the bar for righteous living very high; his expectations for the way believers ought to be living and how they ought to relate to one another are extremely difficult. Actually, the word that first comes to my mind is "impossible."

If your reaction to what we have discovered in the book of James is similar to mine, let me make a few final observations.

First, we ought not to be surprised that we are challenged when confronted with the truth of the Scriptures. It is not for nothing that Jesus is pictured, in the book of Revelation, as having a double-edged sword coming out of His mouth; most commentators see this as a reference to the potent force that His words can be in our lives. And that makes perfect sense. When we look into the mirror of Scripture, especially when we go there with a heart willing to hear God's voice speaking into our lives, we can expect to be humbled and challenged by how far our sinful lives fall short of the righteous perfection that is God's standard, His expectation for the lives of His children. He calls us as believers to be His ambassadors in this world, reflecting His image to everyone who encounters us. When people see us, they ought to walk away feeling like they've had a personal encounter with the living God. I don't say this to discourage you, of course. I just think we often need to be reminded that God expects us to be perfect; He expects us to be holy, because He is holy. And when we honestly confront that standard, which is affirmed and expounded throughout Scripture, it is only natural that we feel convicted. In one sense, that is what the words of Scripture are there for: to teach us and remind us of how far we fall short of who we ought to be and how we ought to live as followers of Christ and children of the King of kings.

And I think, in a nutshell, that is what James is trying to point out. The controversies that surround this epistle serve, I think, as distractions to the larger issue that James is aiming for: we're not living like we should! Though this sounds harsh and uncompromising to our modern ears, the fact of the matter is that we (speaking of the Church as a whole, of course) do not come even close to living up to the standard that God raises for us in Scripture. In so many ways, we fall short of righteous living. And even worse, most of the time, we're okay with that. Most of the time, we are not working to move closer toward that standard; in fact, if we are brutally honest with ourselves, I suspect that most of us would have to admit that, more often than not, we are actively resisting anything that calls us to move closer to that standard. We are happy right where we are.

That is why books like this epistle from James are dangerous, like I warned you in the beginning of this commentary. James is not willing for the children of God to remain children. He wants us to grow up! And the challenges that we find throughout his epistle call us, encourage us, to do just that. And we need to be like the crowd in Jerusalem on the first Pentecost; when they heard what Peter was saying they were **"deeply distressed"** and responded by crying out, **"What should we do, brothers?"**

James has a good answer to that question: grow up! Don't be satisfied with whatever level of righteousness you currently have in your life. Go deeper! Seek, through meditation and prayer, to delve even deeper into the wondrous life that the Spirit of God opens up to all of us as children of the King. Always be looking for ways to make your faith practical, to live out what you believe through genuine acts of love and service to those around you. Strive to be all that Christ has called you to be as His ambassador to this fallen world.

Is this easy? Not a chance! It is perhaps the hardest challenge you will ever accept in your life, and chances are we will never actually achieve this goal of living as Christ calls us to live in every area of our lives. But that doesn't mean we shouldn't continue striving for it, because even though we fail, it is still a goal worth chasing after. And through the power of Christ, who can do all things, you might be surprised at how far He will help you to go!

---

[1] Scripture quoted by permission. Unless otherwise noted, all Scripture verses are quoted from the NET Bible® copyright ©1996-2006 by Biblical Studies Press, L.L.C. http://netbible.com All rights reserved.

[2] Adam Clarke's Commentary: Preface to the Book of James (electronic copy included in the Power Bible CD software)

[3] See John 7:5

[4] Unless otherwise noted, all definitions of Greek words taken from Strong's Greek Dictionary (electronic copy included with *The Power Bible* CD software).

[5] Unless otherwise noted, all references to Warren Wiersbe are taken from: *The Wiersbe Bible Commentary: New Testament*, Cook Communications Ministries, 2007 (electronic edition)

[6] Unless otherwise noted, all references to Charles Tyree are taken from: Tyree, Charles. *James: The Righteous Life that God Requires*, Christian Publications, 1999

[7] Introduction to the Book of James, *King James Study Bible*, electronic edition included in Libronix Digital Library: The Ultimate Bible Study Collection

[8] *Matthew Henry's Commentary on the Whole Bible*: James 1:2 (electronic edition included with the Power Bible CD software)

[9] Weirsbe prefers this alternate, equally valid translation of the word James uses

[10] *Matthew Henry's Commentary on the Whole Bible*: James 1:2 (electronic edition included with the Power Bible CD software)

[11] Lewis, C. S. *The Weight of Glory*. William B. Eerdmans Publishing Company, Grand Rapids, MI. 1949, page 2.

[12] *Adam Clarke's Commentary*: James 1:6 (electronic edition included with the Power Bible CD software)

[13] *Matthew Henry's Commentary on the Whole Bible*: James 1:6 (electronic edition included with the Power Bible CD software)

[14] In this context, fidcuial recumbency means "the act of leaning on God with complete and utter trust"

[15] *William Burkett's Notes on the New Testament*: James 1:6 (electronic edition included with the Power Bible CD software)

[16] *Albert Barnes' New Testament Commentary*. James 1:6 (electronic edition included with the Power Bible CD software)

[17] *Robertson's New Testament Word Pictures*: James 1:6 (electronic edition included with the Power Bible CD software)

[18] *The Believer's Bible Commentary*: James 1:9, electronic edition included in Libronix Digital Library: The Ultimate Bible Study Collection

[19] Rain Forest International School, or RFIS. Check us out on the web at www.rfis.org if you want to know more about us!

[20] Matthew 6:13 and Luke 11:4

[21] *Albert Barnes' New Testament Commentary*: James 1:13 (electronic edition included with the Power Bible CD software); emphasis in original

[22] *Matthew Henry's Commentary on the Whole Bible*: James 1:13 (electronic edition included with the Power Bible CD software)

[23] As Paul admonishes us to do in Philippians 4:8

[24] *The Believer's Bible Commentary*: James 1:12, electronic edition included in Libronix Digital Library: The Ultimate Bible Study Collection

[25] Lewis, C. S. *Mere Christianity*. Barbour and Company, Inc: New Jersey. 1952. P. 78

[26] *Matthew Henry's Commentary on the Whole Bible*: James 1:16-17 (electronic edition included with the Power Bible CD software)

[27] *Albert Barnes' New Testament Commentary*: James 1:19 (electronic edition included with the Power Bible CD software)

[28] *Albert Barnes' New Testament Commentary*: James 1:19 (electronic edition included with the Power Bible CD software)

[29] *The New Dictionary of Thoughts: a Cyclopedia of Quotations*. Edwards, Tryon, editor. Standard Book Company, 1965. All quotes in this chapter are taken from pages 553 - 562

[30] *Matthew Henry's Commentary on the Whole Bible*: James 1:27 (electronic edition included with the Power Bible CD software)

[31] *Albert Barnes' New Testament Commentary*: James 1:27 (electronic edition included with the Power Bible CD software)

[32] Granted, if we accept the likely early date of the epistle of James, then none of the epistles of Paul had been written when James wrote this letter, but I think the point still stands in spite of this.

[33] Joshua 2:9

[34] Joshua 2:11

[35] Joshua 2:9

[36] *King James Study Bible*, James 3 (electronic edition included in Libronix Digital Library: The Ultimate Bible Study Collection)

[37] *Albert Barnes' New Testament Commentary*: James 3:15 (electronic edition included with the Power Bible CD software)

[38] *Albert Barnes' New Testament Commentary*: James 4:4 (electronic edition included with the Power Bible CD software)

[39] *Albert Barnes' New Testament Commentary*: James 4:5 (electronic edition included with the Power Bible CD software)

[40] MacArthur, John. "The Blasphemous Sin of Defaming Others, Part 1." Grace to You Ministries. Found online at http://www.gty.org.

[41] Collins American English Dictionary. Online: http://www.collinsdictionary.com/dictionary/american/slander.

[42] *Albert Barnes' New Testament Commentary*: James 4:13 (electronic edition included with the Power Bible CD software)

[43] Ibid.

[44] *Albert Barnes' New Testament Commentary*: James 4:15 (electronic edition included with the Power Bible CD software)

[45] I thought it worth noting that the NET reverses the typical order of these two words; in most other versions, such as the NIV and the King James, for example, the phrase which the NET renders as "lived indulgently and luxuriously" is "lived on earth in luxury and self-indulgence." Since I don't read Greek, I can't determine which reading is closer to the original, so I will deal with these words in the order in which they are found in the NET.

[46] Adam Clarke's Commentary: James 5: 4 (electronic copy included in the Power Bible CD software)